A Camp Counselor's Manual
for Leaders of
Older Elementary Children

Rejoicing
with
Creation

Tom Malone

Published for the Cooperative Publication Association

John Knox Press
Atlanta

Library of Congress Cataloging in Publication Data

Malone, Tom.
   Rejoicing with creation.

   (Resources for Christian outdoor education)
   Bibliography: p.
    1.   Church camps—Handbooks, manuals, etc.
2. Church work with children—Handbooks, manuals, etc.
I. Title. II. Series.
BV1650.M34   259   79-87747
ISBN 0-8042-1420-4

Contents

Art by Ruth S. Ensign

61778

Introduction

Welcome to the world of summer church camping with older children! You are most likely reading this book because you will be participating in some way in a summer camp program for older elementary children sponsored by the church. This book has been prepared to help you in planning what you and your girls and boys will do together during your time at camp.

Part One of the book gives some background information with which all workers in a summer church camp for older elementary children should be familiar. Chapter 1 explores the purpose of the summer camp as a part of the total Christian education ministry of the church. Chapter 2 spells out the philosophy of small group camping upon which this book is based and talks about how you will function as a leader in this type of camp. Chapter 3 discusses the numerous possibilities for program activities during camp and gives you some criteria for choosing which activities to use. Chapter 4 gives suggestions about how to prepare for your time at camp.

Part Two includes three study themes. The committee responsible for planning the program for your camp will probably designate one of these three themes for use by all groups during your time at camp. You should find adequate material in the chapter on any one of the three study themes for helping you and your children grapple with what the Bible has to say to you today about the theme. You will also find a variety of other activities suggested that will help you and your campers plan for your total camp experience.

Part Three is a resource section with activities and material that will be used with all three study themes.

Part One
Purposes and Planning

1
The Church Camps

It is early June, and school is out for the summer. Books, pencils, and lunch boxes have been put away until next fall. Fred and his best friend are discussing their summer plans. As we listen in, we learn that Fred's plans include attending a seven-day session at Deerskin, a camp owned and operated by the denomination to which Fred's family belongs.

If we could talk with Fred we would learn that the decision to attend Deerskin was not completely his own. Fred heard about Deerskin from Mr. and Mrs. Taylor, his church school teachers. They had talked about summer camp at Deerskin off and on during the winter months. One Sunday in the spring they had asked several older students in Fred's class to tell what they had done at Deerskin the summer before.

Mr. Jones, the pastor at Fred's church, had dropped by Fred's house in early April to bring a brochure describing the program at Deerskin and a registration form. Mr. Jones had talked with Fred and his parents about Deerskin and about what a week at the camp could mean for Fred. On several Sundays after his visit, Mr. Jones had asked Fred whether or not he had decided to go to Deerskin this summer. He was very excited the Sunday that Fred brought his completed registration form by to be signed.

Fred's parents, too, had given Fred much encouragement. After hearing the director from Deerskin speak at a special congregational supper, they were impressed with the program at Deerskin and realized what a growing experience it could be for Fred. It was probably the gentle but persistent encouragement that he had received from his mom and dad that had finally persuaded Fred to give Deerskin a try this summer.

Why all of this excitement about church camp? Why did Mr. and Mrs. Taylor, Mr. Jones, and Fred's mom and dad feel that it was so important to encourage Fred to attend a session at Deerskin?

Answering questions such as these will force us to deal with an even more basic question, "Why is the church involved in camping at all?" That is the question which this chapter will attempt to address. It is important that you understand what the church is about in church camping, so that you can do your part to see that these purposes are accomplished in the camp of which you will be a part.

Why Is the Church Involved in Camping?

The basic, underlying philosophy of this camp leader's manual is that church camping is a part of the church's total program of Christian education. This philosophy implies that the purpose and the goals of church camping are the same as the purpose and the goals of the Christian education program of the church. Robert Davis, in *Church Camping,* defines the purpose in this way: "...that all persons may respond to God in Jesus Christ, grow in daily fellowship with him, and meet all of life's relationships as children of God."[1] This philosophy also implies that the church camp program should be designed to support, complement, and supplement the other programs of Christian education offered by the church.

But above all, such a philosophy implies that the church camp should provide opportunities and experiences that cannot be carried out elsewhere in the church's Christian education program. It is because the church camp does make possible some unique opportunities for learning about and growing in the faith that camping is considered a valid part of the church's ministry. Specifically, this means that the church camp takes advantage of the two important features that are unique to the camp setting—the resources of God's world and the opportunities afforded by the twenty-four-hour-a-day laboratory experience in living that camp provides.

Much—maybe too much—of the church's Christian education program has been centered in the classroom. Church camping moves education out of the classroom and seeks to utilize the resources of the out-of-doors to teach girls and boys about the wonder and vitality of the world and the greatness and majesty of the God who created the world.

Christian educators have long recognized the important part that the environment plays in teaching and learning. "The room teaches!" is emphasized repeatedly in curriculum materials and in teacher training workshops. In the same way, we can affirm: "The world teaches!" Most people have only scratched the surface of what they can learn from God's world.

Church camp provides a unique opportunity for campers and their leaders to explore and learn from the world about them. The world becomes the classroom where campers are encouraged to see, to taste, to smell, to hear, and to touch so that they might come to appreciate the world a little more and so that they might come to know a little better the great and loving God who created such a magnificent world.

Educators have also affirmed the importance of situational teaching as one of the most significant methods of communicating the faith. Many Christian educators would insist that situational teaching is probably the most effective method of teaching in the church, because in situational teaching the Christian faith is applied immediately to the situations and incidents that occur in the lives of the students.

In the camp setting, as campers and their leaders live together twenty-four hours a day, many opportunities arise for the mature Christian counselor to share what the faith has to say about life as it is really being lived. Reconciliation becomes not just a biblical or theological concept to be explored in a study session; it becomes real when Sue and Karen talk over their differences with the help of their counselor and become friends again. Love and acceptance are expressed in action when the small group reaches out to quiet, shy Sandy and makes him feel important and included. Campers and counselors begin to understand something of the dignity of persons as they realize that their common life together is greatly enhanced when they use the gifts and talents that God has given to them so that chores and tasks get done. Christian community is felt, not just talked about, as the small group lingers around the last night's campfire. As the alert counselor helps campers reflect on their life together, the Christian faith becomes alive and relevant.

Camping does have a place in the overall Christian education program of the church, as we begin to see the unique possibilities and potentialities of campers and leaders living together in the context of the Christian community in the world God has made. We must do our best to see that these possibilities and potentialities are realized.

Why a "Church" Camp?

We have discussed the uniqueness of camping as a part of the total Christian education program of the church, and we have affirmed the validity of camping as a part of the church's Christian education ministry. It is important that we say a word about what distinquishes the church camp from the camps sponsored by other agencies and groups.

On several occasions the author has heard a camp leader he admires affirm that church camping is unique because we have the gospel. That statement is not as simple as it first appears. On first hearing the statement, we tend to understand that what makes the church camp different from other camps is that Bible study and worship are added to the list of daily activities. Nothing could be further from the truth! Simply adding Bible study or worship or other "religious" activities does not make a camp Christian.

Instead, a camp becomes a Christian camp when the gospel begins to influence the whole life and atmosphere of the camp. A camp becomes Christian when the teachings of the Bible and the Christian faith become the foundation upon which the entire camp program is built. A camp becomes Christian when the teachings of the Bible and the Christian faith make a difference in people and their attitudes and behaviors.

In such a camp, Bible study is important, not because it is something that we feel we must do since our camp is Christian, but because it is something we want to do because we are Christians. Worship becomes important, not as another activity to include in our already overcrowded schedule, but as a joyous response to the God whom we have come to know in the Bible and through the people and the world about us.

The gospel can make your camp Christian primarily as you and the other leaders who will serve with you are willing to live and communicate the faith that is yours. This is your opportunity and your privilege as a camp leader.

REJOICING WITH CREATION

2
Small Group Camping

We have looked at why camping is included as a part of the church's total program of Christian education. This chapter will focus on one particular kind of camping.

A basic assumption underlying this camp leader's manual is that small group camping is the most effective style of camping for use with older elementary girls and boys. This chapter will seek to define for you what small group camping is all about and how you will function as a leader in such a camp.

The Nature of Small Group Camping

In small group camping, campers are organized into small groups of from eight to ten campers with two co-counselors, one man and one woman. As much as possible, the small group should be composed of an equal number of boys and girls. Each small group will function as a separate, autonomous group within the general guidelines and objectives of the particular camp. Each group of girls and boys and their counselors will be responsible for planning and implementing most of the activities in which the group will be engaged. Each small group should have a designated area for its own use. Here the group will live, work, play, worship, and study. Suggestions for how to develop your small group living area are given in Chapter 9 of the resource section of this book. The small group area should be accessible to the two sleeping areas—one for the boys and their leader and the other for the girls and their leader. These two sleeping areas should be as close together as possible.

In your camp, there will probably be from four to six small groups. The ideal number seems to be four small groups totaling approximately forty campers, and the absolute maximum should be six small groups totaling no more than sixty campers. You will spend most of your time in small groups, but there will be occasions when two or more small groups or maybe even the entire camp will join together for certain activities such as for meals in a central dining hall or for a total camp worship service. Experience has proven that total group or inter-group activities should be limited, particularly during the early days in camp. How often you participate in total camp activities will be determined by policies set by your director and/or camp committee.

Why Small Group Camping?

Girls and boys of elementary age need opportunities to develop close and meaningful relationships with other children their own age, and they need the security of continuing and satisfying relationships with mature adults. Small group camping provides the setting for just such relationships to occur as campers and leaders share life together twenty-four hours a day.

Elementary girls and boys also are able to begin taking responsibility for their own lives and the lives of others. Camp, particularly in the context of the small group, provides unique opportunities for the girls and boys to have a share in planning their activities and carrying them out. They learn that the needs, interests, and concerns of each individual are important and must be considered. And, they learn that they must do their part because the group is depending on each of them to make his or her contribution.

In small group camping, real life problems of living together, getting along with others, and working for the good of the group and with each other are all present. These situations occur because of the very nature of people. There will be situations that will try both your patience and your resourcefulness so that you are thrown back again and again to the Source of strength and wisdom. However, these human relationships are among the most important elements of the camp environment. Where else but in the Christian community can people whose imperfect attitudes and immature behavior are known to one another still work together and develop mutual understanding and love for one another? In such an environment, persons are able to learn and change and grow in a community in which each member may enter into intimate, sustained, and redemptive relationships through which God can work and in which every person can serve and be served.

The Leader's Role in Small Group Camping

As you prepare for leadership of a small group, you need to consider what it is that you will do as a leader in a small group camp. Your basic responsibility will be to guide a group of eight to ten girls and boys. You will be a part of a team, sharing the task of leadership with your co-counselor and the girls and boys themselves. You will be a part of a total camp staff, and you will abide by the rules and policies set up by a director or camp committee, and you will work within the framework or guidelines established by the director or committee.

The style of leadership you practice will vary during your time in camp. At times you will be an autocratic leader with rigid bounds and rules, particularly when the health and safety of the campers are at stake. At other times you will function as a laissez-faire leader with few or no bounds and rules, particularly as you seek to help the campers assume responsibility for the life of the camp group. Hopefully, you will function most frequently as a democratic leader who works with the group to set its own goals and to determine the best way to accomplish these goals.

You must remember that older elementary girls and boys will need a lot of help and guidance from you and your co-leader. Too much freedom and responsibility will overwhelm them. These children function best in choosing from alternatives, not in determining the alternatives. You and your co-leader will need to assume major responsibility in guiding the group. You will consider your group at all times and will let your plans develop out of the life experiences which you share with the campers. You should involve the campers in planning whenever possible. Talk over your plans with them and give them choices in schedule and activities.

In your work of guiding a small group, you will share life with your campers twenty-four hours a day. As you move through various activities during a camp day, you will be an organizer, a teacher, a guide, a parent, a resource person, but always you will be a friend. The responsibility of functioning as a small group leader is an awesome task, but it is a task that offers you unique opportunities to mold the lives of children and to share with them the faith that is yours. The rewards of the task far outweigh the responsibility.

OBSERVABLE RESPONSES	IMPLICATIONS FOR TEACHERS
Mental	
Have improved skill in reading to learn instead of learning to read.	Books, audiovisuals, maps, and similar resources can be used in many learning activities.
Can understand time and distance —history, geography.	Can profitably study history, biography, and geography of the church. Great leaders, life of Christ, and the spread of the church across the world become important. The Bible begins to make sense, for students can understand that Jesus lived before Paul, Moses before Jesus, etc.
Can calculate—with figures, problems, issues.	Plan activities that involve reasoning and thinking through issues and problems.
Have beginning ability to do abstract thinking. Begin to understand concepts such as love, truth. Enjoy mystery.	Teaching activities may include implications for the future—for instance, social and political changes that may be required in society; introduction of new concepts. Children can make decisions and understand they will be expected to hold to them awhile.
Are capable of organizing and seeing relationship between various facts, experiences, people.	Time lines and other activities in which facts and ideas learned earlier can be put together in relationship and perspective are now possible.
Are capable of intense and lengthy mental involvement while body is relatively inactive, such as watching TV for long periods.	Though body still has the need to be active, teacher may expect longer period of concentration and study. Learners may be expected to work on their own or provide assistance to one another.

OBSERVABLE RESPONSES	IMPLICATIONS FOR TEACHER
Physical	
Intensely active, must be physically involved.	Though child can be still for longer periods, inactivity cannot be overdone. Games, use of the outdoors, learning centers in which movement is permitted, are essential.
Enjoy games of all sorts: physical sports, table games, card games.	Fellowship events may include all sorts of sports and games.
Are interested in own bodies: muscles, weight, height, strength.	Learning about stewardship of one's body is highly important.
Social	
Have strong sense of what is fair and unfair.	Provide opportunities for judgment, decision-making, and evaluating.
Develop intimate relationships of lasting value. Are great hero worshipers: sports persons, movie stars, TV persons. Imitate heroes. Generally responsive to guidance of adults.	Be alert that learners might tend to worship teacher and follow literally guidance and suggestions.
Are capable of intense emotion: outbursts of anger, clinging love. Enjoy companionship — playing games together. Have tendency to cling to friends of own sex, perhaps to tease other sex.	Encourage children to group themselves, selecting others with whom they wish to work. Avoid forced mixing of sexes in work projects, but likewise avoid frustrating it.
Love animals and accept them as personal friends. Collect intensely—cards, insects, coins, junk, posters.	Provide opportunity to share interest in pets and hobbies.

Who Are Your Campers?

Since you will be sharing life so intimately with older elementary children (generally fifth and sixth graders), it is important that you understand all you can about what these children are like. Try to find an opportunity to visit with a group of older elementary children for a while at a school or club or at your church school. Talk with them about what it is they like to do and what it is that they are interested in exploring and talking about. Then study carefully the chart on pages 16 and 17. Compare the information in the chart with what you have learned from your visit. Finally, consider carefully the implications of what you know now about older elementary children for your planning for your time at camp.

3
The Camp Program

We have looked at why camping is included as a part of the church's total program of Christian education. We have focused on small group camping and how you will function as a leader in this style of camping. This chapter will look at the camp program, what children and leaders do during camp. It will be brief and will simply present an overview of camp program. The chapters in Part Two of the book will present specific activities to be used in developing each study theme.

What Do We Do in Camp?

Camp "program" is difficult to define, for basically "program" refers to everything done in the camp from the time the first camper arrives until the last camper leaves. The camp program includes Bible study, worship, and hiking; but it also includes the conversation that campers and counselors enjoy as they walk to the dining hall or the spontaneous water fight that occurs as campers are washing up for bed. Everything that happens at camp has the potential for helping the child grow and learn.

Any day in camp will consist of both planned and unplanned activities. The sum total of all of the planned and unplanned activities that occur in the daily life of a group constitutes the camp program. You as a small group leader must prepare carefully before camp for the planned activities, but you must also be very alert during camp to see that you and your campers are able to learn from the spontaneous, unplanned activities. Sometimes just as much significant learning takes place from the spontaneous activities that occur and are dealt with by an alert counselor as takes place from those activities for which we so carefully prepare.

A Philosophy of Program

Many factors shape the program for a particular group. The overall objectives and policies of a camp, the physical setting of the camp, the facilities and resources available at the camp, the weather and climate, and the interests and skills of both counselors and campers all affect the direction of the program of a small group of campers and leaders. The program develops and grows out of the resources available within the people who make up the group and within the camp setting.

Generally, in a small group camp, each small group is free to build its own program and schedule. Any planning done, of course, should be consistent with the overall objectives of the camp and should fit within the broad framework which has been set up by the director or the camp committee. The framework will generally designate times for meals, for sleeping and rest periods, and for all-camp activities such as campfires, vespers, or recreational activities. The large blocks of remaining time are left to the small groups to utilize as they wish.

You and your co-leader will generally need to plan for the first day in camp, but by the first evening the campers should be ready to participate in the planning with you. As leaders, you must be careful to allow the campers to develop a program which grows out of their interests and needs. You, however, are a part of the small group, and you should feel free to contribute to the planning and to serve as an advisor, counselor, and resource person. After you get to know the members of your group and their interests and needs, you will know more about how to help them plan a program that is right for them.

Possible Program Activities

There are virtually unlimited possibilities for camp program activities. Some activities are necessary for people living together, such as cleaning the cabin or shelter and setting the tables at meals. Other activities are an important part of an experience in the out-of-doors, such as campfires and nature study. Still other activities, such as swimming and playing games, are done primarily because they are fun. And finally, certain activities such as Bible study and worship are done because of who we are and what we are about in this Christian education program called camping.

Possible program activities can include the following:

Bible study
Worship
Group planning and evaluation
Music
Recreation
Projects
Water activities
Camp chores
Outdoor living skills
Creative art activities
Creative writing activities
Exploration of the natural world
Crafts
Conversation

Criteria for Selecting Activities

How do you choose from the many activities that you read about in this and other books and that you and your campers generate yourselves? The following questions may give you some guidelines to follow in evaluating whether or not an activity should be included in the camp program you are planning:

1. Will the activity help you accomplish the overall objectives of your camping program?
2. Is the activity one that can best be done in an outdoor setting, or could it be done better in a church school setting?
3. Is the activity one that can best be done at a *church* camp?
4. Will the activity encourage participation of your total small group rather than just a few individuals?
5. Will the activity help develop a sense of community and group consciousness?
6. Will the activity help provide variety and balance to your overall program?
7. Will the activity help your campers grow and learn in some significant way (in understanding, in confidence, through learning a new skill)?
8. Is the activity one that a majority of the campers will want to do and will enjoy doing? (Remember: Camp should be fun!)

A Word of Caution

As you can see, the possibilities of things to do in camp are endless. Enthusiastic elementary girls and boys tend to plan too many things to do. The schedule becomes hectic as the group rushes from one activity to another without really taking time to enjoy them.

One of your primary responsibilities as a small group leader will be to help your group plan wisely and to follow through on their planning. Elementary campers need the sense of achievement and accomplishment that comes from really doing a task well. You will need to help them pace themselves so that this can occur.

A Planning Chart

As you and your campers plan your days, you will need to arrange the various activities that you decide to do in some logical sequence. Many leaders find that using a small group planning worksheet, such as the one on the next page, is a helpful way to assist campers in planning. The planning worksheet encourages a group to plan according to three major blocks of time each day rather than according to an hour-by-hour schedule. Remember that your pace should be leisurely and relaxed, so be realistic as you and your campers fill in the chart about how much time various activities are going to take.

It is good to balance active experiences with some that are more relaxing. Don't forget that your campers need some time to do things of their own choosing, either individually or with two or three others (supervised, of course).

Finally, remember that your planning should be flexible. Help your campers realize that they can adjust the schedule if the need arises. One of the joys of small group camping is that you don't have to be slaves to a schedule.

A Typical Day

To give you an idea of what a typical day could look like in a camp with older elementary children, a sample schedule is given on page 24. Remember, however, that your schedule should grow out of what you and your boys and girls decide to do in your particular camp. This is only a sample of one day's schedule in one camp with one small group of campers and leaders.

REJOICING WITH CREATION

WORKSHEET FOR SMALL GROUP PLANNING

WEEK OF ————

	Monday	Tuesday	Wednesday	Thursday	Friday	Saturday
MORNING						
AFTERNOON						
EVENING						

Morning	Breakfast
	Morning worship
	Clean cabins
	Walk to small group living area
	Bible study and discussion
	Continue work on living area
	(lash serving table, gather firewood)
	Lunch
Afternoon	Rest hour
	Plan for Wednesday's cookout
	Swim
	Supper
Evening	Outdoor games
	Campfire (singing, stories, discussion, marshmallows)
	Prepare for bed
	Evening worship in cabins

Planning <u>for</u> the Program

How do you prepare to be a leader in a small group camp where the campers will have a say in planning? You should be aware by now that you will not prepare or plan the program for your small group. Instead you will plan *for* the program. There is a difference. If you plan the program, then you write down before camp begins exactly what your group will do each hour of every day. Planning the program leaves no opportunity for campers to help shape and mold the program. The program belongs to you, the leader, and not to the group. The program may meet many of the needs and interests of the campers in your group, or it may not.

When you plan *for* the program, however, you think through and write down in a small notebook or on index cards many activities and experiences which your group could have. You think of possible ways to explore your theme in worship and Bible study. You write down songs your group could sing, games they could play, craft ideas they could make; but you wait to let your campers have a say-so in the final decisions. Because of your advance preparation, you will have many ideas to suggest. As you get to know your campers' needs and interests better, you will know which activities will be best to suggest to your particular group.

It is much easier to plan a camp program than to plan *for* one. But the values of a program which grows out of the needs and interests of campers

6 1778

and counselors together make the extra work worthwhile. The next chapter will give more suggestions about how to plan *for* your time at camp.

Special Days

In addition to your overall planning for your time at camp, you will need to prepare for some special days. The following discussion should help you in planning for these special times.

THE FIRST DAY

The first day of camp is very special. The campers have been looking forward to this day for a long time, and the staff has been preparing for this day for an even longer time.

You and the other leaders should arrive in camp at least one day before your campers arrive. This will give you an opportunity to orient yourself to the camp, and it will give you plenty of time to get comfortably settled in your cabin or shelter before the first camper arrives.

You will probably meet your campers at the cabin or shelter after they have registered. As the campers arrive, greet them and their parents. Do all you can to make each one of the campers feel welcome and comfortable. Introduce each camper to the other campers in the shelter, and help each one find a bunk and begin to feel comfortable and at home in the new surroundings.

Chatting with parents will help to put them at ease about their children's well-being at camp. Just be sure that conversations with parents do not keep you from greeting and putting at ease other campers who arrive.

Suggesting that all campers wait until everyone in the shelter has arrived to unpack is a good idea. It eliminates the embarrassment of a well-meaning parent wanting to make up a camper's bed, and it puts the campers on their own from the very start.

It is helpful to have some things to do while your campers are waiting for others in the shelter to arrive. You can have native materials on hand so campers can make simple name tags or bunk cards. Or you may want to help the campers build a miniature model of the camp from a map you provide, using sticks, stones, and earth. Simple refreshments are always good, and those who arrive early can help to prepare the refreshments for those yet to come.

When all of the members of your small group have arrived, meet together and play a game or two to help campers learn names and start to get acquainted. It is usually a good idea to take a tour of the camp so that campers will start to learn their way around. During the tour you may have an opportunity to introduce the campers to some of the staff people who will be working with them during the week—the director, the lifeguards, resource people, kitchen staff, and maintenance staff.

After supper, a campfire is always a good way to get further acquainted, have some fun, and begin planning for the week. You will want to spend some time at the campfire introducing the study theme for your session.

Allow plenty of time to get ready for bed on the first evening. Prepare the campers for any night sounds which may be new and strange to them. Assure the campers that you wish to be awakened if any of them needs you for any reason. A good story told or read by the counselor will help the campers get to sleep.

SUNDAY IN CAMP

As you and your campers make plans for Sunday, you will want to plan for times of worship, fellowship, and rest. You will need to talk with your director about any plans for all-camp activities on Sunday, such as an all-camp worship service or trip. If such activities are scheduled, it is hoped that they will be planned by camper representatives from all of the small groups.

RAINY DAYS

Rainy days can spoil an otherwise good camping experience unless counselors have planned for them. Every counselor should plan some imaginative activities that will make rainy days into stimulating, different days that may well be the highlight of the camp session. For the most part, activities should go as planned when it is raining. You may need to have some of them under a tarpaulin or in a shelter.

You will certainly want to take advantage of some of the unique opportunities afforded by the rain. Rain hikes are always fun. Help your campers observe how different the world looks, smells, feels, and sounds in the rain. You can make a rain gauge and measure the rainfall. Do anything that you can to help your campers begin to look upon the rain as the friend that it is and not an enemy.

If the weather is too stormy to be outside, there are almost endless possibilities of things to do inside. This list will suggest just a few to start your thinking: write letters, do some housekeeping in the cabin or shelter, work on some craft projects, practice campcraft skills, play games, plan a cookout, sing and learn new songs, read or tell stories, plan skits and have a skit show, or plan a worship service.

In addition to worship, your activities for the day may include a longer rest period with time for writing letters and visiting within the shelter group, an opportunity to visit other small group living areas, a picnic supper which would permit the kitchen staff to have Sunday evening off, and churning homemade ice cream. Use your imagination to make Sunday a special day in camp!

THE LAST NIGHT

Some time should be spent on the last night at camp in helping the campers reflect on the experiences they have had in camp and on what these experiences have meant and can mean to them in their lives. Such reflection should be done in a meaningful but natural way. The experiences themselves are what should be remembered, not an emotional mood as they were talked about. Help your campers think through the answers to questions such as these: What has the camping experience meant to me? What have I learned through the various activities at camp? How have I grown in my understanding of what being a Christian is all about?

The evening's discussion should be closed with a brief period of worship. Again, you will not try to create an emotional mood. Sing some of the group's favorite songs. Read some of the Scripture passages that have been meaningful to the group. Close with a time of prayer in which you and any of the campers who wish can thank God for your time together at camp.

THE LAST DAY

The last day in camp is often hectic, but it should not be. Help your group to schedule plenty of time for packing and putting the camp in order. Also, allow some time for saying "good-byes" to new friends and for collecting addresses. Be sure to encourage each of the campers in your shelter group to check out with you, so that you will know when and how each camper leaves. Be sure to be on hand yourself to see each of your campers off.

4
Preparing for Camp

By this point in your reading, you will have begun to understand the significant place that camping plays in the church's overall program of Christian education. You will have also begun to understand what the program is like in a small group camp and how you will function as a leader in such a camp. This chapter will help you focus on how you can prepare to serve as a leader in camp.

Your preparation will be of three kinds. You will do your personal preparation; you will participate in the training sessions offered by the director of your camp or by the camp committee; and you will plan with your co-leader.

Regardless of your past experience and training, you will want to prepare anew for your time in camp. Take full advantage of every opportunity that is provided so that you will be prepared to fulfill your task faithfully and effectively.

Personal Preparation

Nothing can take the place of good personal preparation before camp begins. You will find that you will have little or no time for preparation once the campers arrive. Adequate planning and preparation before camp begins will free you to enjoy your campers and to devote yourself fully to making camp a happy and meaningful experience for them.

You will certainly want to study very carefully this counselor manual and any other printed resource materials provided by your director or camp committee. After reading the introductory material in Part One of this book, you will want to study very carefully the theme chapter from Part Two which will be used in your particular camp. You will want to study in some detail the Bible passages that you will use in conjunction with this theme. Commentaries and other biblical reference books can be borrowed from your minister or church library if you have questions about any of the passages. You will also want to become very familiar with the material in the resource chapters in Part Three of this book.

After you have done your initial reading, you will want to begin making specific plans for particular parts of your camp program. It is very helpful if these specific plans are written down in a small notebook or on index cards. Separate pages in your notebook or separate index cards should be made for such program ingredients as these: (1) get-acquainted activities, (2) songs, (3) games, (4) stories, (5) nature activities, (6) Bible study suggestions, (7) craft ideas, and (8) worship ideas. You may want to include page numbers from this book or other resources if you think you will need to review any material before using it in your camp session.

Remember that you need to list many more ideas than you will be able to use. This will allow you to make choices about which activities, games, songs, or whatever will best fit your group of campers. A well-thought-out card file or notebook will be an invaluable resource for your use at camp.

In addition to your reading and the preparation of a card file or notebook, you will want to prepare yourself for camp in two additional ways. First, you will want to learn all you can about older elementary girls and boys. Reading about the characteristics of these children will help, but you will also want to spend some time with children of this age. Visitation of a church school or public school class will help you better understand what these children are like and how they learn. Take the opportunity to talk with children of this age to find out what it is they do and do not like to do and about how they like to learn.

And finally, you will need to practice some of the skills you need for camp. Practice tying knots, lashing, and building fires. You might even enjoy taking some friends or your family on a cookout in order to practice building a fire and preparing a meal.

Pre-Camp Training

Your camp committee or director should provide at least two training events for you and the other members of the camp staff. The first session should be held several months prior to the opening of camp and the other during the twenty-four to thirty-six hours prior to the opening of camp.

These training sessions should be held at the camp site and should provide many opportunities for the staff to have small group experiences in the out-of-doors. Whenever possible, staff members should have the opportunity to learn by doing, particularly camp skills.

The pre-camp training should offer all members of the staff the opportunities to:

—discuss together the importance of church camping as a part of the church's overall program of Christian education;

—learn about the policies and procedures to be used in their particular camp;

—become familiar with the facilities and natural resources of the camp;

—find out what equipment and supplies are available and when and how they are to be issued to small groups;

—participate in a camping experience, including a cookout;

—learn basic camping skills;

—learn songs, games, and other activities to use with the campers;

—participate in worship and Bible study experiences similar to those which will be used with the campers;

—learn about the resources available in the camp library;

—plan with their co-leaders.

The final training session just prior to the opening of camp is a very important time. All members of the staff should be present and should get comfortably settled in their cabins or shelters. Activities should be planned that continue to mold the staff into a group. The time will be spent coordinating plans and getting everything ready for the arrival of the campers. You will need to be sure that you get yourself and all of your materials and supplies in order, so that your campers come into a relaxed and reassuring atmosphere when they arrive.

Planning with Your Co-Leader

As soon as your director or camp committee recruits all of the staff, you should be notified with whom you are to work as a co-leader. You and your co-leader will want to spend a significant amount of time together planning for your session at camp. Time should be set aside in the pre-camp training sessions for you to do this, but you may also want to schedule additional time for planning.

You will want to spend time getting to know each other and getting to know the particular skills that each of you brings to the camping experience. You will want to talk about how you will work together during the camp and about who will take the major responsibility for various activities. You will talk about how you will function as a team where each person supports and complements the efforts of the other person. You will also talk about how you will involve the children in your planning, so that they, too, become a part of the team.

You will want to prepare very carefully for the Bible study and for ways in which the study theme can be woven into every area of camp life. You will want to work out detailed plans for your first day in camp, including how you plan to get acquainted with the campers and how you plan to help them get to know each other. You will want to look at ways to evaluate your camping experience each day and ways that you and your campers will plan for the next day.

And finally, you will work out assignments for who is to do what specific things in preparation for camp. You should make a list of what materials and supplies you will need and who will secure them.

Part Two
Themes

5
Belonging

Why This Theme?

To belong is a basic need of people. We spend much of our time and energy in life seeking to become a part of various groups, to "belong" to these groups. Older elementary children especially feel the need to belong, to be accepted, to be a part of the gang. The need to belong affects their behavior, their attitudes, and even the way they dress.

Belonging is also a major emphasis of the Christian faith. Perhaps no concept or idea gets to the heart of the biblical message as does the concept of "belonging." The Bible tells the story of God and of a people who belong to God and to each other in a special way.

The activities suggested in this study chapter will provide you and your campers many opportunities to explore what it means for us as Christians today to belong to God, to each other, and to the world God has given us. Keep the theme constantly before yourself and your campers so that you may all come to feel closer to one another, to the world, and particularly to God as you share life together at camp.

Main Ideas

The following main ideas will be explored in the teaching/learning activities for this study theme:

—To belong is a basic need of people.
—The Bible tells the story of a group of people who belong to God, to

each other, and to the land in a special way.
—We belong to this special group of people.
—Our belonging implies responsibility to God, to each other, and to the land.
—We can rejoice and celebrate because we belong.

Getting Started with the Campers

The first day in camp provides an excellent opportunity to begin to explore and to experience what it means to belong. The activities chosen for this first day should focus on helping the campers get acquainted with each other and with you, helping them get comfortably settled in their shelters, and helping them begin to feel at home with the camp setting itself. The activities suggested below will help accomplish these three purposes. Choose the activities that you feel will fit your particular group and your camp setting, and feel free to supplement these activities or to substitute others in their place.

Remember that the first few hours with your campers are very important and can help set the tone for your entire time together. Do all you can to make your campers (many of whom will be away from home and family for the first time) feel welcome and a part of the camp community.

1. Have supplies on hand at the shelter for making name tags. An activity such as this helps each camper to get involved from the very beginning and provides a context for you and your campers to begin to get acquainted.

2. When all of your campers have arrived, spend some time getting unpacked and settled in the shelter. This helps campers begin to feel secure and a part of the camp.

3. When you get your entire small group together, play a game to get acquainted and to learn names.

4. Take a walk around the camp to help orient campers to the various buildings and facilities so that they will start to feel a part of the camp.

5. Visit the staff people at the camp who will be working with your campers in various capacities (kitchen staff, waterfront staff, resource people, the director) to help campers begin to feel a part of the larger camp community.

6. Play some games together. Remember that your purpose is to start

developing a sense of "belonging," so avoid games which eliminate people.

7. Enjoy a campfire together. A small campfire will be sufficient. Gathering close around a small fire will help draw the group together. Sing, tell a good story, continue to get acquainted and to learn things about each other, and plan for the next day.

8. Conclude your campfire with discussion and worship. Begin to introduce the theme of "Belonging." Ask the campers to tell about various groups to which they belong. Ask what it feels like to belong. Ask in what ways they have felt like they belonged since they have been here at camp. Emphasize that we will spend our time at camp exploring and experiencing what it means to belong. End the day with a worship experience which celebrates the fact that we do belong. Use Psalm 100, emphasizing verse 3, which celebrates the fact that we belong to God. Close with a brief prayer, thanking God for this new community of people here at camp to which we belong.

How to Develop the Theme

The days in camp will give you many opportunities to explore in depth what it means to belong. Study of biblical passages will help interpret what is actually being experienced in the lives of you and your campers about what it means to belong to God, to the land, and to each other.

You should work throughout the week on activities that will help to develop a sense of belonging to the group. Real Christian community does not often happen unintentionally. We have to work to make it happen, and the most effective way to do that is to provide a variety of projects and activities for the group to work on together.

Three major emphases are included below to help you and your campers focus on belonging. Spend as long on each emphasis as your time in camp will permit. Notice that there are many activities suggested that can be used throughout the day to explore the implications of the Scripture for your life together. Do not confine your study to just one study period each day, but instead try to help your campers understand that the teachings of the Bible speak to all of life.

We Belong to God

The introductory session focused on belonging, how people feel when they belong or are a part of a group and how they feel when they do not belong or are not a part of a group. This part of the study will begin to explore this whole idea of belonging a little more, particularly emphasizing the fact that we belong to God.

Belonging is a major theme of the Bible. The Bible tells the story of God and a people who belong to God in a special way. This special relationship between God and a people had its beginning in the covenant which God made with Abraham. God renewed the covenant with Abraham's descendants and with the entire Jewish nation. We Christians believe that we, too, are a part of this special group of people who belong to God.

The Bible study for this emphasis will focus on *Genesis 12:1–5*. Here are some suggestions for proceeding with your study:

1) Ask any campers who can to define the word *covenant*. The dictionary defines a covenant as an agreement between two or more persons. In a covenant, both parties agree to certain things.

2) Ask the campers to give some examples of covenants or agreements that people make with one another today. They may suggest such things as law covenants, building covenants or contracts, marriage covenants, the covenants or contracts between an employer and employees, and promises or covenants which two people make to do something for each other or to keep a secret.

3) Tell the campers that long ago God made a covenant with Abram. Give them some background information on Abram. Abram was the son of Terah, a man who lived in the ancient southern Mesopotamian city of Ur (present Iraq) almost 2,000 years before Christ was born. Terah moved his family to the northern Mesopotamian city of Haran (in present-day Turkey). Making the journey with Terah were his son Abram, Abram's wife Sarai, Terah's grandson and Abram's nephew Lot, and all of their servants and slaves. A short time after the family settled in Haran, Terah died; and his son, Abram, became the head of the family. It was while Abram was living in Haran that God made a covenant with him.

4) Have the campers read individually the story of God's covenant with Abram in Genesis 12:1–3 to find the answers to these questions:
   a. Who started the covenant, God or Abram?
   b. What was Abram to do? Do you think this would be easy? Why or why not?
   c. What did God promise to do for Abram?

5) After the campers have had time to read the passage and think about the questions individually, discuss the questions as a group.

6) Have the campers read Genesis 12:4–5 to find out if Abram kept his part of the covenant.

7) Discuss with the campers the implications of keeping the covenant for Abram and his family. Once again they were going to have to pack up all their belongings and move, leaving behind friends and family and familiar surroundings. If there is time, the following simulation might help to impress upon the campers the significance of what God was asking Abram to do.

Pretend that your small group is Abram's family: Assign parts to Abram, Sarai, Lot, the servants, etc. You have just finished your evening meal, and the family is sitting around the campfire. Abram tells about his conversation with God and what God is asking him to do. How do you think the conversation would have gone?

8) Be sure to emphasize to the campers that we, as Abram's descendants, are included in the covenant and thus belong to God in a special way just as Abram did.

9) Conclude the study by letting the campers individually write short prayers expressing to God the joy they feel because they are part of God's covenant people. Have one or two campers read their prayers to conclude the study.

RELATED SCRIPTURE PASSAGES

Genesis 17:1–8 (God renews the covenant with Abraham in Canaan.)
Psalm 95 (The psalmist expresses joy at being part of the covenant family.)
Micah 6:6–8 (The prophet talks about our relationship to God.)

ADDITIONAL ACTIVITIES

1. Dramatize Sarai or Lot saying "good-bye" to their best friends as they leave Haran.
2. Let the campers pretend to be Lot: Last night around the campfire your Uncle Abram announced that you were going to leave Haran to go to a land which God would show you. You really didn't understand the whole matter. Write a letter to your best friend expressing your doubts and confusion.
3. Have a group discussion on what is implied when we today say we belong to God. Remember, Abraham and his family had to travel a great distance. What is required of us?
4. Plan for your campers to have some time alone to consider what it means for them personally that they belong to God.
5. Talk together about times when members of the group have felt especially close to God.

6. Let the campers plan a worship service which celebrates the fact that we belong to God. Perhaps several campers could present one of the dramatizations prepared earlier. Other campers could read their letters or their prayers.
7. Begin learning the song, "They'll Know We Are Christians by Our Love."

We Belong to Each Other

People who belong to God and enjoy a special relationship with God also belong to each other. Just as belonging to God requires something of us, our relationship with other people requires something of us, too. Jesus' parable of the good Samaritan gets to the very heart of what our relationships with other people should be like. The suggestions given below will help you and your campers study Jesus' parable from *Luke 10:25-37.*

1) Talk with your campers about the context of the parable. Jesus told the parable of the good Samaritan in the context of a conversation with a teacher of the Jewish law who asked Jesus several questions. The lawyer was one of those people in Jesus' day who were concerned with keeping each one of the tiny requirements of the law of Moses. Unfortunately, this lawyer, as did many of the lawyers, seemed to enjoy arguing about little points of the law more than he did actually living by the law. Thus, he was ready to debate with Jesus the issue of just who the neighbor was that he was to love.

2) Have the campers read Luke 10:25-37. The following exercise will help them to get the details of the story in mind: Pretend that you were a passerby on the road from Jerusalem to Jericho and saw the incident. Compose a telegram to send to your home describing how the man who was beaten was treated by all of the other characters in the story. Treat the story as a historical event but use your own words and phrases. Each letter space in the telegram costs three cents. Limit your spending to $4.00 on the telegram.

3) Ask those campers who will to share their telegrams.

4) As a group, discuss each one of the characters in the parable and what each person was like. For each character, name a kind of person or a group of people who would be the equivalent today of that character.

—The *priests* represented the highest order of professional religious leaders among the Jewish people.
—The *Levites* were laypersons who served as assistants to the priests and were responsible for the care of the Temple.

40   REJOICING WITH CREATION

—The *Samaritans* were a mixed race of people living in Samaria, the area to the north of Judah. Many of the Samaritans did not follow the law and worship of the Hebrews, and they were not considered by the Jews as worthy of association.

5) Divide your campers into groups of three or four. Let those in each group pretend that they are reporters for a modern newspaper. As a group, have them rewrite the parable in terms of life today. They can use people or groups of people in their communities as the setting.

6) Have each group read its parable to the total group. After each presentation, ask the question: "Is this modern parable true to the sense of Jesus' parable?"

7) Discuss the following questions:
   a. What is the main point of the parable?
   b. What are the implications of the parable for us today?
In the parable, Jesus teaches that our neighbor includes any person we encounter in life who needs our help. We are to help without questioning the worth of the character of those we encounter, and we are to help even those people who have brought trouble on themselves as the traveler had done by carelessly traveling the dangerous road alone. Also, our help must be practical. Feeling sorry is not enough. Our help must require some activity on our part.

The implications of the parable for us today are obvious. We, too, are to "Go, and do likewise." We are to meet the needs of all of those people we encounter in life who need us.

8) To summarize, have each person complete the sentence: "According to Jesus' teaching in the parable of the good Samaritan, a neighbor is...."

9) Conclude the study with prayer.

RELATED SCRIPTURE PASSAGES

1 Samuel 20:1-42 (David and Jonathan's love for each other.)
Philippians 2:19-30 (The companionship of Paul, Timothy, and Epaphroditus in the work of spreading the gospel.)

ADDITIONAL ACTIVITIES

1. Continue learning the song, "They'll Know We Are Christians by Our Love."
2. Have a discussion on what it means that we belong to each other.

3. Have each camper draw the name of another camper to observe for the day. Campers are to observe the good things that this person does during the day. Have a time to share the observations, perhaps around the campfire at the close of the day.
4. Encourage each person in your group to do something special or nice for the camper they are observing. The campers are not to know who is doing the nice things for them.
5. Is there someone in your group who needs special help or who seems to be a little lonely? Is there someone who is having trouble keeping up with the rest, or someone who may feel neglected or left out? Ask one or more of the campers to give some special attention to this camper during the day.
6. Share an experience with another group in camp to begin developing the feeling of belonging to a larger group. Take a hike, share a cookout, or have a campfire together.
7. Lay out a "treasure hunt" for another group to follow. At the end of the treasure hunt, leave directions for the group to join your group for refreshments, maybe watermelon or homemade ice cream.
8. Have an echo sing across the lake.
9. Have an all-camp worship service to which each group contributes. This will begin to develop a sense of belonging to the whole group.
10. Let your group make a centerpiece for their table in the dining room.
11. Let your group make signs giving your group name to put around your tables in the dining hall and outside of your cabins or shelters.
12. Read the story, "The Porcupine Whose Name Didn't Matter," from *The Way of the Wolf* by Martin Bell. The story emphasizes the point that friends don't have to do anything; they just have to be there.

We Belong to the Land

Both of the accounts of creation in Genesis (Genesis 1 and 2) include the gift of the land to Adam and Eve. Both accounts put the responsibility on them to care for the land. Genesis 1 describes this in terms of subduing the earth and having dominion over the creatures. Genesis 2 speaks of cultivating and caring for the earth. Both accounts carry the implication of being good stewards of the land which is a gift from God.

When God made the covenant with Abraham and his family, the covenant promises included the gift of the land. Thus, the people who were to have a special relationship to God were to also have a special relationship to the land.

We who are among the descendants of Abraham enjoy this special relationship to the land even today. And, just as belonging to God and to each other requires something of us, so, also, belonging to the land requires something of us. We, like Adam and Eve, are to care for the land.

The Bible study for this emphasis will be *Genesis 2:4b–25*. The activities suggested below will challenge you and your campers to think and to act more seriously about caring for the land.

1) Genesis 2 may well have been a story told around the campfire as Hebrew children asked the question, "How did the world begin?" Pretend that you are a group of Hebrew nomads (wanderers) sitting around the campfire. You have spent the day enjoying the beauty of God's world. The youngest member of your group asks, "Just how did the world begin?" Everyone gets very quiet as grandfather clears his throat for a story. Listen to what he says. Read Genesis 2:4b–25 in a modern translation, such as the *Good News Bible*.

2) Talk with the campers about this particular story of creation. Remind them that the Bible is not a scientific textbook. In fact, the writers lived in a pre-scientific age. Their concern was to tell about the Creator and his relationship to his creatures and especially to the people he had called to be his family. So, the account in Genesis will not answer the scientific question, "How?" Instead, it will tell us "Who?" and "Why?" Science will be able to tell us more and more about just how the world was created, but the more we learn about the marvels of this magnificent world, the more we stand in awe of the God who created it all.

3) Ask your campers what Genesis 2 says about the importance of people. What is the significance of verse 15? What are the implications of this verse today?

4) Compare Genesis 2:15 with Genesis 1:26 which says that humankind will have dominion over the earth. In what ways are the two verses saying the same thing?

5) Discuss together the ways in which we have succeeded and the ways in which we have failed in caring for the earth. (We have cultivated and cultivated, but have we guarded the land?)

6) Take a short hike around your camp property to observe ways the natural resources have been cared for and ways they have been wasted or misused. Look for some ways that your group can fulfill the obligation placed on us in Genesis to care for the land. Choose a conservation project for your group to complete together during your time at camp. Check with the director before proceeding.

7) Conclude your study by writing a prayer that includes thanksgiving for the world God has made, confession for our misuse of the natural world, and a request for guidance on how to use responsibly God's gifts to us.

RELATED SCRIPTURE PASSAGES

Genesis 1:26-31 (Man and woman as the climax of creation are to have dominion over the creation.)

Genesis 17:1-8 (God's covenant with Abraham and his descendants included the gift of the land.)

Psalm 8 (Man and woman are to have dominion over all of creation.)

Leviticus 25:1-7 (Each seventh year was to be a "sabbatical year," and the land was not to be planted.)

Leviticus 25:8-12 (Every fifty years, a "year of jubilee" was to be celebrated, and the land was to rest and be treated as a gift from God.)

Leviticus 25:23 (The land belongs to God, and we are strangers and sojourners.)

ADDITIONAL ACTIVITIES

1. Take a hike to enjoy the land around camp. Maybe this hike could be an Acclimatization "Quiet Walk." (See pages 59-73 in *Acclimatizing,* by Steve Van Matre.)
2. Plan an exploration trip around your camp property to observe ways the natural resources have been wasted or misused, to see effects of erosion, to observe results of drought or fire, or simply to enjoy the beauty of God's world.
3. Study the hymn, "All Creatures of Our God and King."
4. Illustrate the hymn, "All Creatures of Our God and King."
5. Do some Acclimatization exercises. (See *Acclimatization* and *Acclimatizing* in the bibliography.)
6. Use some of the natural materials you find around camp to create something. The "Nature Crafts" chapter in the resource section will give you some suggestions.
7. Do a leaf rubbing.
8. Draw "Then and Now" pictures showing the results of people's exploitation of natural resources. An example would be a picture that shows a thickly wooded forest and a landscape with a sparsity of trees.
9. Have the campers make a frame by cutting a rectangular hole in an index card, leaving an inch and a half all the way around. The campers can then use the frame to focus in on an area around them. Have them jot down a list of things that are particularly pretty in that scene and a list of things that take away from the beauty of the scene.
10. Pretend that you are an object in the natural world. Write a letter to people expressing your sadness over what they are doing to you and your sisters and brothers. (St. Francis called the creatures his "sisters and brothers.")
11. Read or tell the legend of Jonathan Chapman:

Not Even an Apple Core[3]

Jonathan Chapman felt sorry for a little girl who cried because she didn't want to go West when the apples were getting ripe. It made him feel lonely, too, to think of living without any apple trees. There would be no pretty blossoms in the spring and no apple butter, no cider, and no apple pies to eat.

"Don't cry," Jonathan promised her. "I will plant thousands of tiny seeds in the wilderness. Apple trees will grow in Ohio, Illinois, Indiana, and Kentucky." He kept his promise. As he walked through the countryside, he planted apple seeds here and there, making a tight brush fence around them to conserve the moisture.

Everyone saved apple seeds for Jonathan. The cider mill was his best source of supply. It is said that when he was picking the seeds out of the apple mash and putting them in his sack, a boy taunted him, calling "Johnny, Johnny Appleseed." The name stuck with him.

Johnny was a queer-looking sight wearing his gunnysack coat, his books stuffed in the front of it. On his head his stewpot hat kept him protected from the sun. He never wore any shoes and carried no weapons to protect him. Wherever he went, he carried a large sack of apple seeds on his back.

All the settlers were delighted to see Johnny, for he brought news from the villages. After visiting awhile, he would ask, "Now do you want to hear some news from heaven?" He'd take out his Bible and read his favorite verse found in Ecclesiastes 11:6, "In the morning sow your seed, and at evening withhold not your hand; for you do not know which will prosper, this or that, or whether both alike will be good." Then he always added, "It is God who giveth the increase."

In a village in Indiana one time a hornet crawled up Johnny's pants leg and stung him. Johnny carefully pushed the hornet down his pants leg and told it to fly away home.

"Why didn't you kill the hornet?" asked a friend. "Why," Johnny replied, "it was defending itself with its God-given sting. I haven't the heart to step on a worm, kill a snake, or beat a dog. Each loves life in its own way, as much as you do, as much as I do."

Some say apple trees which sprouted from seed Johnny dropped still burst into blossoms, provide leafy shade, and produce juicy fruit—all the work of a lonesome man who never threw an apple core in his life.

12. Let the campers share stories they have heard of other women and men who loved the out-of-doors and helped others to enjoy the world God has made.

Concluding Your Study

We belong! You and your campers have only been able to scratch the surface of just what that statement means. It may be that your experiences together at camp have helped to deepen your understanding of the privileges and the responsibilities implied in our belonging to God, to each other, and to the land. As you and your campers return to your homes and churches, you will go with new understandings and new commitments to fulfill your responsibilities to God, to the world, and to other people.

On the last day of camp, you will want to review in some way the study you have done. The following activities will help you do that:

1. Divide your campers into three groups. Let each group review the Scripture passages you studied in each of the three major emphases. Ask each group to choose one or two key verses which they think summarize what they learned in that emphasis.

2. After a few moments, let one person from each group share the verse or verses the group has chosen and state why the particular verse or verses were chosen.

3. Ask any campers who will to share what they have learned during their time at camp about what it means to belong.

4. Let the campers summarize what they have learned by doing one of the following activities:

   a. Complete the sentence, "Belonging is. . . ."
   b. Write a cinquain poem using "Belonging" as the title.
   (A cinquain poem contains five lines. Line 1 is the title. Line 2 contains two words which describe the title. Line 3 contains three words which can either be three action words or a phrase about the title. Line 4 contains four words and describes a feeling about the title. Line 5 contains one word which refers to the title.)

5. Ask any campers who will to share their completed sentence or their cinquain poem.

6. Join hands in a circle and sing together "They'll Know We Are Christians by Our Love."

7. Close with a time of prayer during which you and some of your campers express thanks for the fact that you belong to God, to each other, and to the land.

6
Brokenness and Healing

Let there be peace on earth and let it begin with me;
Let there be peace on earth, the peace that was meant to be.
With God as our Father, brothers all are we.
Let me walk with my brother in perfect harmony.
Let peace begin with me, let this be the moment now.
With every step I take, let this be my solemn vow:
To take each moment and live each moment in peace eternally.
Let there be peace on earth and let it begin with me.

Why This Theme?

We live in a world of broken relationships. Nations are at war with nations. Races are in conflict with other races. Individuals are constantly in conflict with other individuals. Even within many families, brokenness prevails as marriages end in divorce and as parents and children live in constant conflict with each other.

Older elementary children are very much aware of the brokenness around them. They are the children of fighting parents. They themselves experience conflict with their siblings, their parents, and their friends. They are aware of the larger community and world conflicts because of television, radio, and newspapers.

Because of the broken relationships evident in the world around them, the church needs to speak a word to its children about healing. What better place is there to do this than the camp setting? This study unit will explore stories of brokenness and healing from the Bible. These stories will deal with brokenness between people and between people and God. The activities suggested will give some clues to you and your campers about just how you can heal the conflicts and broken relationships with other people and with God that you experience in life.

Main Ideas

The following main ideas will be explored in the teaching/learning activities for this study theme:

—People are separated from God and from other people by broken relationships.
—Broken relationships cause pain and hurt.
—It is possible to heal broken relationships.
—There is much joy and happiness when broken relationships are healed.

Getting Started with the Campers

As always, the focus of your activities on the first day should be on helping the campers get settled in their shelters and on helping them get acquainted with you, with each other, and with the camp itself. Remember that your first few hours with your campers are very important. Do all that you can to make your campers (many of whom will be away from home and family for the first time) feel welcome and comfortable in the camp community.

The following activities are suggestions of things to do on the first day of camp. Choose the activities from this list which best fit your camp setting and your particular group of children. Feel free to supplement these activities or to substitute others in their place.

1. As your campers arrive at the cabin or shelter, let them make name tags. Such an activity gets the campers involved from the very start and provides a context for conversation which will help the group get to know each other and you more quickly.

2. Serve simple refreshments at the shelter as the campers arrive. Those who arrive early can help prepare the refreshments for others in the group.

3. After all of your campers have arrived, let them unpack and get settled in the shelter so that they will begin to feel comfortable in the camp setting.

4. Bring the boys and girls in your small group together and play a game to help them get acquainted and to learn names.

5. Take the entire group on a tour of the camp. Introduce them to the staff people who will be working with them during their time at camp.

6. If there is time, go swimming or play a game together just for fun.

7. After supper, you may want to have a campfire. Sing, continue to get acquainted, tell a good story, and begin making some preliminary plans

for the next day and for the entire camp session.

8. As you conclude your campfire, begin to introduce the theme of "Brokenness and Healing." Ask the campers to share incidents in their own lives or in the lives of their friends where there has been a broken relationship. Ask how they felt while the relationship was broken. Ask them to share how the relationship was finally healed. Ask how they felt when the relationship was healed. Tell the campers that you will be studying the stories of some people from the Bible whose relationships with others or with God were broken and then healed.

9. End the day with worship. Read Psalm 32, which expresses the sadness the psalmist felt when his relationship with God was broken by sin and the joy he felt when he confessed his sin and his relationship with God was healed. Close with a brief prayer.

How to Develop the Theme

The theme of "Brokenness and Healing" will be explored through the use of three stories from the Bible. The story of Jacob and Esau and the story of Joseph and his brothers will be used to explore the theme of brokenness and healing among people, and the parable of the lost son will be used to explore the theme of brokenness and healing between a person and God. It is hoped that studying the experiences of these biblical characters will help you and your campers deal with the situations of brokenness and healing that you encounter in your lives.

You are encouraged to spend as long on each one of the three biblical stories as your time in camp will allow. There are many activities suggested in each section to help your campers learn as much as possible from the biblical stories. Use these activities throughout the day or over a period of several days.

You will also find that many activities are suggested that can be used throughout the camp day to explore the implications of the Scripture passage for your life together. Use these activities to help your campers begin to understand that the teachings of the Bible speak to all of life.

Jacob and Esau

Jacob and Esau were the twin sons of Isaac and Rebekah. They were different in many ways, but both of them were very selfish and self-willed. Their selfishness brought about a broken relationship between these two brothers which was not healed for many, many years.

The story of the two brothers is told in several chapters of Genesis. We will look at some of the key passages of their story in the suggestions which follow:

1) Divide the campers into two groups. Each group will look at one of the two major incidents that brought about the broken relationship between the two brothers. One counselor can work with each group.

Group I will study the story of Jacob stealing the birthright from Esau.

(1) Ask the campers to read individually the story from Genesis 25:27–34.
(2) Let one of the campers summarize what happened.
(3) Give the campers some background information on the birthright. The "birthright" consisted of the special rights and privileges of the firstborn or oldest son, which were the receiving of a larger inheritance and the right to be the head of the tribe.
(4) Discuss together the significance of what Esau had done. He had given up the rights which were his by birth.
(5) Discuss together who was at fault. Remember that Jacob bribed Esau with food in a weak moment when he was hungry, but Esau gave in to his weakness.
(6) Prepare to share what happened and the significance of the action with the total group when you come back together.

Group II will study the story of Jacob deceiving his father and cheating Esau out of his father's blessing.

(1) Ask the campers to read individually the story from Genesis 27:1–37.
(2) Let one of the campers summarize what happened.
(3) Give the campers some background information on the blessing. The last words of a dying man were very important to the Hebrews. These words were considered to be prophetic, and they could not be taken back. They were also legally binding. Thus, the pronouncement of a father's blessing was extremely important.
(4) Discuss the significance of what had happened. Jacob had tricked his father and cheated his brother.
(5) Prepare to share what happened and the significance of the action with the total group when you come back together.

2) When both groups have completed their study, let them share with each other what they have learned.

3) As a result of these two incidents, Esau became very angry. Have one of the campers read Genesis 27:41–45 aloud to the group to find out what happened.

4) Jacob lived in Haran for many years, but finally he decided that he must return to his homeland in spite of Esau's anger in order to take up the responsibility placed on him by his acceptance of the birthright.

5) Esau, instead of remaining angry with his brother about the past, was happy to see Jacob. Have one of the campers read the story of the healing of their relationship aloud from Genesis 33:1–11.

6) Discuss together how you think Jacob and Esau must have felt after their broken relationship was healed. Maybe some of the campers will be able to share stories of the joy they have felt when a broken relationship has been healed.

7) End your study with prayer.

ADDITIONAL ACTIVITIES

1. Dramatize some part of the story. Different groups could work on different scenes from the story of the life of these two brothers. After each dramatization, let the campers talk about how they would have felt following that particular incident.
2. Let the campers pretend they are Jacob: Today you have cheated your brother, Esau, out of your father's blessing. Take a piece of paper and a pencil. The paper is your diary. Write down your feelings about the day. Let any campers who will share what they have written.
3. Let your campers pretend they are Esau: Today your brother, Jacob, has cheated you out of your father's blessing. Take a piece of paper and a pencil. The paper is your diary. Write down your feelings about the day. Let any campers who will share what they have written.
4. Discuss what it feels like to have an important relationship broken for some reason.
5. Discuss what it feels like to have a broken relationship healed.
6. Let the campers make a charcoal drawing of one of the scenes in the story.
7. Let the campers make a craft item to give as a gift to someone with whom they have had a broken relationship.
8. Let the campers plan a worship service based on the Jacob and Esau story. Perhaps some of the campers could present one of the dramatizations prepared earlier. Other campers could read their diary sheets. Still others could write prayers or choose hymns which would be appropriate.
9. Begin learning the song, "Let There Be Peace on Earth."

Joseph and His Brothers

Jacob had twelve sons. Of these, Joseph and Benjamin, the two youngest, were his favorites because they were the sons of his favorite wife, Rachel, and because they were born to him in his old age. The other brothers became particularly jealous of Joseph, and they finally became very angry with him.

The story of Joseph and his brothers also covers several chapters of Genesis. The following suggestions will help you study the key passages in this story.

1) Divide the campers into two groups. Each group will look at one of the main reasons why the jealousy between Joseph and his brothers grew to the point where the relationship between them was broken.

Group I will study the story of Joseph and the coat that his father gave him.

(1) Ask the campers to read individually the story from Genesis 37:3–4.
(2) Ask the campers why they think the brothers became angry. Was it because of the coat or because they felt that their father loved Joseph more than them?
(3) Discuss together whether or not you feel the brothers had a right to be angry with Joseph.
(4) Prepare to share the story with the other group when you come back together.

Group II will study Joseph's two dreams which made his brothers angry.

(1) Ask the campers to read individually the accounts of the two dreams in Genesis 37:5–11.
(2) Ask the campers why they think the brothers became angry.
(3) Discuss together whether or not the brothers had a right to be angry with Joseph.
(4) Prepare to share the story with the other group when you come back together.

2) When both groups have completed their study, let them share what they have learned with the other group.

3) Have one or two of the campers read Genesis 37:12–28 aloud to find

REJOICING WITH CREATION

out what happened as a result of the anger of the two brothers.

4) The travelers carried Joseph to Egypt where he lived for many years. Joseph became a very important person and was placed in charge of the food supply of Egypt.

5) Many years later, there was a shortage of food in Joseph's home country, and his brothers came to Egypt to buy food. Joseph recognized his brothers and after testing them and finding out that they had changed, he told them who he was. Have one of the campers read the story of how healing took place between Joseph and his brothers from Genesis 45:3–15.

6) Discuss together why healing was able to take place between Joseph and his brothers. Was it because Joseph had changed, or because his brothers had changed, or because all of them had changed?

7) Be sure to point out to the campers the great joy that Joseph and his brothers felt when healing took place between them.

8) End your study with prayer. Include thanksgiving for the relationships in the lives of you and your campers which have been healed in the past and ask God to heal the broken relationships that still exist in the world.

ADDITIONAL ACTIVITIES

1. Let the campers use natural dyes from flowers and grasses to paint a picture of Joseph's decorated coat.
2. Let the campers discuss situations in which brokenness has occurred in their lives because of jealousy.
3. Let the campers discuss times in their lives when they have experienced forgiveness. Was there as much happiness as in the Joseph story?
4. Many parts of the story of Joseph and his brothers lend themselves to dramatization. Maybe different groups of campers will want to prepare to dramatize different parts of the story.
5. Let the campers pretend that they are one of Joseph's brothers: Today you have sold your brother, Joseph, into slavery in Egypt. Write a page in your diary describing how you feel about what you have done.
6. Allow time during the day for campers to write a letter to someone with whom they have experienced a broken relationship. Encourage them to say things in their letter which will help heal the broken relationships.
7. Let the campers plan a worship service based on the story of Joseph and his brothers. Again, dramatization and writing done earlier could be incorporated into this service. Maybe another small group could be invited to join you for this service.
8. Continue learning the song, "Let There Be Peace on Earth."

The Parable of the Lost Son

Jesus told the parable of the lost son to illustrate the love and the grace of God. It is a happy story because it ends with an illustration of a broken relationship between a person and God being restored. The following activities will help you lead your campers in a study of what this parable, found in *Luke 15:11-24,* teaches us about brokenness and healing:

1) First, you will want to help your campers get the story in mind. We will consider the story in three scenes.

The first scene is described in Luke 15:11-12.
(1) Have one of the campers read these verses aloud to the group.
(2) Let the campers discuss what might have prompted the younger son to make this request of his father.

The second scene is described in Luke 15:13-20a.
(1) Have one of the campers read these verses aloud to the group.
(2) Let the campers discuss how they think the father must have felt as he watched his younger son leave home.
(3) Then, let them discuss how they think the son felt in the early days in the far country and after all of his money was gone.
(4) Talk together about why the son did not decide to return to his father's home sooner.

The third scene is described in Luke 15:20b-24.
(1) Have one of the campers read these verses aloud to the group.
(2) Let the campers once again discuss how the father felt and how the son felt in this scene.
(3) Point out to the campers that the father had no obligation to the son once he left home. He accepted him back simply out of his great love for his son.

2) Tell the campers that Jesus told his parable to teach people about God and God's love. The father in the parable represents God, and the younger son represents a person who turns from God and lives in sin.

3) Discuss together what the parable teaches us about God. This parable is often called the "parable of the loving father." Ask the campers if they think this is a good title. Why or why not?

4) Discuss together what the parable teaches us about people. Remind the campers that we do not have to do something big to separate ourselves from God. Little things separate us, too.

5) Finally, discuss what the parable teaches us about healing our broken relationships with God. The parable teaches us that God wants to heal broken relationships because God loves people. If this is true, then who stands in the way of such relationships being healed?

6) End your study by letting the campers write prayers confessing the things which separate them from God and asking God to forgive them so that the relationship between them can be healed.

ADDITIONAL ACTIVITIES

1. Let a group of the campers rewrite the parable of the lost son in modern terms.
2. Let a group of campers dramatize one or more scenes from the parable.
3. Let the campers pretend to be the younger son: You have wasted your money in the far country. You are now broke and hungry. Write a letter to your best friend back home describing your situation and asking what you should do.
4. Let the campers pretend to be the father: Your son has been gone for several months now, and you miss him very much. You are talking with your best friend about the situation. What would you say?
5. Let the campers make a list of the alternatives which the younger son faced when his money ran out. Let them talk about the advantages and disadvantages of each alternative. Ask them if they would have made the same choice that the younger son did.
6. Let the campers draw a charcoal sketch of the father watching his son walking down the road to the far country.
7. Let a group of campers write a song based on the parable of the lost son. They could write the words to fit a tune they all know.
8. Help the campers plan a worship service which celebrates the fact that our broken relationships with God can be healed. Utilize the creative work that the campers have done earlier.

Concluding Your Study

We live in a world of broken relationships, but there is the possibility for these relationships to be healed. It is hoped that you and your campers can affirm this statement after your study of the theme of "Brokenness and Healing" during your session at camp. As you and your campers return to your homes and churches, you will carry with you new insights about what causes relationships to be broken and a new sense of hope that the healing of broken relationships can take place.

On the last day of camp you will want to review in some way the study you have done. The following activities will help you do that:

1. Divide your campers into three groups. Let each group review one of the biblical stories you have studied during camp. Ask each group to write

down the three most important points they learned from that story.

2. After a few moments, let one person from each group share the key points the group has written down.

3. Ask any campers who will to share any other insights they have had about the theme of "Brokenness and Healing" during their time at camp.

4. Let the campers summarize what they have learned by individually completing these two statements:

   a. Broken relationships are caused by....

   b. The healing of broken relationships takes place when....

5. Ask any campers who will to share their completed sentences.

6. Join hands in a circle and sing, "Let There Be Peace on Earth" as a closing prayer.

7
Respond with Joy

Joyful, joyful, we adore Thee,
God of glory, Lord of love;
Hearts unfold like flowers before Thee,
Opening to the sun above.
Melt the clouds of sin and sadness,
Drive the dark of doubt away;
Giver of immortal gladness,
Fill us with the light of day.

Thou art giving and forgiving,
Ever blessing, ever blest,
Wellspring of the joy of living,
Ocean depth of happy rest!
Thou our Father, Christ our Brother,
All who live in love are Thine;
Teach us how to love each other,
Lift us to the Joy divine.

Why This Theme?

There is no quality that ought to be as evident in the lives of Christians as the quality of joy. As Christians ponder what God has done to redeem them through the death and resurrection of Jesus Christ, they ought to be elated. In Christ they are forgiven of their sins and are set free to live a new life of wholeness and joy as God's people.

The Westminster Shorter Catechism states that the highest purpose of a person's life is "to glorify God and enjoy him forever." And since one's relationship to God determines the way that a person looks at others and the natural world, then it naturally follows that the people who seek to glorify and enjoy God will also enjoy the people around them and the world in which they live.

This particular study theme, "Respond with Joy," which is based on Paul's letter to the Philippian church, will offer many possibilities for you and your campers to discover and experience ways in which you may enjoy God, each other, and the outdoor setting in which you are to live for a few

57

days. Let this theme be the basis of your thinking and your living. Let it permeate every part of your life together.

Main Ideas

The following main ideas will be stressed as you explore this theme with your campers. These ideas should grow out of your study of the letter of Paul to the Philippians.

—The Christian life is a life of joy.
—This joy grows out of a person's vital, living relationship with God as that person comes to know God in Christ.
—We can know joy no matter what our circumstances in life if our life is rooted in a relationship with Christ.
—Joy can permeate all that we do and say in life.

Getting Started with the Campers

Your first day in camp will be taken up with getting acquainted with your campers, getting them comfortably settled in their shelters, and introducing them to the camp itself. These activities can be a good introduction to the theme, as you are able to convey to the campers your own enjoyment in being with them and in having the opportunity to work with them during your camp session. You will talk about many of the things that you will be doing together as you take a walk, go swimming, or visit in the shelters while your campers unpack.

Remember that the first few hours with your campers are very important and can help set the tone for your entire time together. Do all you can to make your campers (many of whom will be away from home and family for the first time) feel welcome and a part of the camp community.

The following activities are suggestions of things to do on the first day of camp. Choose the activities from this list which fit your camp setting and your particular group of children. Feel free to supplement these activities or to substitute others in their place.

1. As your campers arrive at the cabin or shelter, let them make name tags. Such an activity helps your campers get involved from the very beginning and provides a context for you and the campers to get acquainted and for the campers to get acquainted with each other.

2. You may want to serve some simple refreshments at the cabin or shelter as the campers and parents arrive. Those who arrive early can help prepare the refreshments for those who come later.

3. When all of your campers have arrived, let them unpack and get settled in the shelter so that they will begin to feel comfortable in the camp setting.

4. Bring the boys and girls in your small group together and play a game to get acquainted and learn names.

5. Take the group on a tour of the camp and introduce them to other staff people. You may want to end the tour at your small group living area to get it ready for your activities there. Talk with the campers about some of the things that could be done in the living area, such as lashing a work table or cooking a meal. If you plan to have a campfire the first evening, you will want to spend some time building your fire area and gathering wood.

6. Spend any other time you have enjoying some games or a visit to the swimming area. Participate with your campers in these activities. They are excellent ways for you to get to know your campers.

7. As you gather after your evening meal (possibly around the campfire), play some get-acquainted games if these are still needed by this time, sing fun and folk songs, or simply share some of your interests and hopes for your week together. This time should not be extended too long since the day has been full and more time will be needed this first evening to get ready for bed.

8. Begin introducing the theme for the week by telling the campers that you will be studying Paul's letter to the Philippians. Tell them this letter has been called the "Letter of Joy," for in the letter Paul has a great deal to say about the "joy" that he has experienced since coming to know Jesus Christ. Read Philippians 4:4–7 aloud to the group and close with a prayer that includes thanks for God's love and for bringing you together at camp.

How to Develop the Theme

The study theme, "Respond with Joy," will focus on portions of Paul's letter to the Philippians. We will begin by studying the account of the founding of this church from the book of Acts. Next we will simulate hearing the letter as if we were members of the Philippian Church who first heard the letter. Our study will then take a close look at three key passages from the letter to see what these passages have to say about the theme of joy.

The Founding of the Church at Philippi

Your first Bible study with the campers will focus on the founding of the church at Philippi. The letter itself will take on more meaning if the campers undersand the circumstances under which Paul founded the church and if they are aware of some of the people who made up the church and Paul's relationship with them.

The story of the founding of the Philippian church is told in *Acts 16:11-40*. Here are some suggestions about how to proceed with the study.

1) Give the campers a little bit of background on the city of Philippi itself and let them locate the city on a map if one is available. The city of Philippi was located in East Macedonia in the northern part of Greece. It was founded by Philip, the father of Alexander the Great, in 368 B.C. The city was located on a major route between Europe and Asia and was thus a great trade and communications center.

2) Have one of the campers read about Paul's vision, which led him to this city, from Acts 16:6-10.

3) Divide the campers into three smaller groups to read the accounts of the people with whom Paul came into contact at Philippi. *Group I* should read the account of Lydia in Acts 16:11-15. *Group II* should read the account of the slave girl in Acts 16:16-18. *Group III* should read the account of the jailer in Acts 16:19-40. Each group should read the verses assigned to them and should discuss the following questions:

   a. Whom is the passage about?
   b. What were these person's relations to Paul?
   c. What was the outcome of their encounters with Paul?

You and your co-leader should move from group to group, helping in any way you can.

4) Bring the entire group back together and let each group report on what they have learned.

5) Let the campers engage in an activity to reinforce what they have learned from this study. Offer them two options and let them choose which they will do.

a) One group of children may like to dramatize a part of the story of the founding of the Philippian church. The scene in the Philippian jail would lend itself well to dramatization.

b) Other children may enjoy doing some creative writing. Let them pretend to be one of the people introduced in Acts 16 and write a letter to a friend telling about Paul and what has happened to them because of him.

6) Let any of the campers who are willing share their letters and let the group working on the dramatazition present it to the total group.

7) Close your study with prayer.

ADDITIONAL ACTIVITIES

1. Let each of the campers pretend to be one of the three characters discussed in Acts 16 and write a first-person account of what has happened to him or her.
2. Let the campers pretend to be the child of the Philippian jailer. What would you tell your best friend about what happened in the jail?
3. Let the campers draw pictures showing some scenes from the early days of the church in Philippi.
4. If a small map is available, let several campers draw a large map and locate Philippi on it.
5. Discuss what it would have been like to have met Paul and to have been a part of the early Philippian church.

You Are There in Philippi

The next session will consist of a simulation in which you and your campers pretend that you are the Christians in Philippi who have gathered for worship and to hear read a letter from your friend Paul.

1) You will need first to give your campers some brief background on the reasons for the letter. Paul was in prison in Rome between A.D. 61 and 63. (Some scholars propose that he was in Ephesus, and some think it was Caesarea, possibly at an earlier date.) He was waiting for God to release him in some way so that he could finish the plans he had for spreading the gospel. The Philippian Christians were concerned about the imprisonment, and they sent greetings and a gift by Epaphroditus, one of the members. While there with Paul, Epaphroditus became seriously ill. Later

the Philippians were concerned over both Paul and Epaphroditus. When Epaphroditus recovered and returned home, Paul sent a letter to the Philippians. There seemed to be at least three reasons for writing: (1) to express to his friends in Philippi his gratitude for their sending their greetings and gifts by Epaphroditus; (2) to encourage his friends who were concerned over his imprisonment; (3) to present the faith in Jesus Christ that would restore a spirit of unity to the church.

2) Set the scene for the simulation as follows:
It is early on Sunday, a working day in Philippi, and you have gathered at the home of Lydia with your Christian friends to worship. The room is crowded. Lydia is standing by the door to usher in the latecomers. The slave girl is there and so are the jailer and his family. Other converts are present. Some are very new and are waiting for the return of Paul or another leader to give them instruction and baptize them. The service has already begun. One of your number has read from the Old Testament. Another person has read an account of the crucifixion and resurrection of Jesus. Now you are all excited because the jailer announces that a letter has come from Paul. The room gets very quiet. You hear him begin: "From Paul and Timothy, servants of Christ Jesus...."

3) You and your co-leader should take turns reading portions of the Philippian letter to give the campers the flavor of this very personal and intimate letter. The following passages would be good ones: 1:1–2; 1:3–11; 1:12–14; 1:19–26; 2:1–11; 2:19—3:1; 4:1–13; and 4:21–23. Choose three or four of these passages to read. Reading from a simpler translation, such as the *Good News Bible,* would be better. Because of the large amount of Scripture, you will need to stop and ask questions for clarification both during and after each section to help the new converts understand. You could also break up the readings by having the group sing appropriate songs between some of the sections. Since Sunday was probably a work day and the Christians were meeting early, they could even eat breakfast while listening to the reading. You could actually do the simulation at breakfast time or around a mid-morning break.

4) End the session by having the group describe and discuss how they think they would have felt if they had been among the early Christians in Philippi who heard Paul's letter read.

ADDITIONAL ACTIVITIES
1. Let the campers pretend they are Paul and write a letter to their home church. What would he say?

2. Let the campers pretend they are the slave girl writing in her diary on the Sunday evening after Paul's letter was read. What would she write in her diary?
3. Let the campers pretend they are Lydia. It is Sunday afternoon, and she is visiting one of the Christians who is ill and was not at the service this morning. What would she tell this person?
4. Let the group plan a worship service modeled after the service at which Paul's letter was read.
5. Let the campers make a charcoal sketch of the church service in Lydia's home.

Joy

The remaining sessions should focus on some key passages from the letter itself. Choose one passage to deal with each day, or smaller groups could study different passages on the same day.

Philippians 1:3-11

1) Ask the campers to read the passage silently to find the answers to the following questions:

a) What is the reason for Paul's joy?

Paul's mood of joy has its roots in his attitude of thanksgiving. He is thankful for the "partnership" in sharing the gospel which he feels with the Philippian Christians. He rejoices in the fellowship and work which he shares with the Philippians because they are bound with him in the service of Christ.

b) What can you learn from this passage about Paul's relationship to the Philippian Christians? How does he feel about them?

Paul had a very close and intimate relationship with the Philippians. This letter reflects great love and affection and concern for them.

c) What effect do you think these words of Paul's had on the early Christians who heard them?

Paul's words must surely have been a source of strength and encouragement to the Philippians.

2) After the campers have had time to read the passage and think about the questions, discuss the questions together.

3) Let the campers paraphrase these verses so that they can really capture the joyous mood of the passage.

4) Have several of the campers share their paraphrases with the entire group.

5) End the study with prayer.

Philippians 4:4–7

1) Ask the campers to read the passage silently to find the answers to the following questions:

a) What does Paul say in this passage about rejoicing?

Twice in the same sentence Paul encourages his Philippian friends to rejoice. This repetition was probably used by Paul to convince the Philippians that joy can accompany trials and afflictions such as those which Paul and the Philippian Christians were experiencing in their lives.

b) Based on this passage, what is the source of Paul's joy?

Paul's joy is "in the Lord." The source of joy for the Christian grows out of that person's relationship with Jesus Christ. Thus, Christians can know joy no matter what circumstances they encounter in life. Paul's own life is proof of this. (Remind the campers that Paul was in prison when he wrote these words.)

c) Paul talks about peace in verse 7. How are peace and joy related?

Paul has just encouraged the Philippians to take all of their problems and requests to God in prayer. They do not have to face their problems alone. God will share them and will fill them with a peace that surpasses their human comprehension. This peace, which is a gift from God, will turn their thoughts once more to Jesus Christ, thus freeing them to live lives of joy and gratitude. Thus, peace and joy are very closely related in Paul's thinking.

2) After the campers have had time to read the passage and think about the questions, discuss the questions together.

3) Let the campers paraphrase these verses.

4) Have several of the campers read their paraphrases.

5) End the study with prayer.

Philippians 4:10–13

1) Ask the campers to read the passage silently to find the answers to the following questions:

a) What is Paul's secret?

He has become *Christ*-sufficient. He has come to depend on Christ as a source of comfort and strength. No problem or adversity is too great for him and Christ together.

b) Why can he boast of being unaffected by outward circumstances?

He has based his satisfaction and happiness in life on a source other than material and physical comforts and pleasures. Thus, outward or physical circumstances have little effect on his inward joy and satisfaction.

c) Who gives him power?

Paul affirms that Christ is his source of power and that he is able to do all things with Christ's help.

2) After the campers have had time to read the passage and think about the questions, discuss the questions together.

3) Talk together about what this passage says to us about our attitude when we encounter problems and trouble in life.

4) End the study with prayer.

ADDITIONAL ACTIVITIES

1. Let your group plan a fun campfire and then invite another small group to join you.
2. Let the group ask the camp director to let them plan a "Game Festival" to be held one afternoon for all the groups to enjoy.
3. Teach your group the hymn, "Joyful, Joyful, We Adore Thee."
4. Let a group of campers write a new stanza to the hymn, "Joyful, Joyful, We Adore Thee."
5. Let a group of campers illustrate the hymn, "Joyful, Joyful, We Adore Thee."
6. Let the campers write prayers of thanksgiving for God's gift of joy.
7. Use the following story some time during the week to give your campers an appreciation of Beethoven's gift of joy to the world.

The Music of a Deaf Composer

Ludwig van Beethoven was the son of a German musician. He was the oldest of three children. He began practicing the piano for long hours before he was nine years of age.

His father expected him to practice the music of great composers and had little patience with Ludwig's interest in composing endless tunes that flowed through his mind and heart.

He had several excellent teachers. Christian Neefe taught him in Bonn, Germany, when he was eleven years old. When he first heard Ludwig play, he said, "You need orderly training. I require a great deal of work, you know." Ludwig replied, "I shall be glad to work hard, sir." It was not long before Mr. Neefe realized that Ludwig had the makings of a genius.

When Ludwig van Beethoven was twenty-eight years old, he became aware that he was getting deaf. He tried to keep this tragic news from his friends. He became angry with his doctor when he was not cured. In his discouragement he withdrew from his friends and they became troubled about him. In fact, he began to feel that life was not really worth living. Then, for some unknown reason, his life was marked by a sudden change. He realized that he should not keep his deafness a secret any longer. So he entered the social life of Vienna again, to the delight of his many friends. As he accepted his deafness, his whole life had a note of triumph. He could still compose music. He said to some of his friends, "I shall accept it as my mission in life to bring beautiful music to the world. For the sake of beauty I can offer others, I shall fight against my deafness."

He composed several beautiful symphonies. We are particularly grateful for his Ninth Symphony. It is glorious music and continues to inspire people all over the world. He gave not only to his friends in Vienna but to the world a priceless treasure of music. When the Ninth Symphony was first played in Vienna in 1824, the people actually shouted for joy. But the deaf composer, who conducted the orchestra that night, had heard the music only in his mind and soul. He knew nothing of the effect on the audience until someone turned him around to see the gratitude and joy of the people. They realized the wonder of Beethoven's gift, unimpaired and even enriched in his affliction.

Henry van Dyke wrote words that have been set to the theme from the choral movement of the Ninth Symphony, "Hymn to Joy." The hymn expresses joy for all God's marvelous works in his giving and forgiving through Jesus Christ. It reminds us of the relation we have to each other because of our relation to Jesus Christ, the Joy Divine.

Concluding Your Study

The Christian life is a life of joy! It is hoped that this affirmation of Paul's Philippian letter has become a part of your thinking and the thinking of your campers. Also, the entire camp experience should have enabled you and your campers to experience the reality of this affirmation. As you and your campers return to your homes and churches, you will carry with you memories of a joyful and happy experience with your Christian friends at camp.

On the last day, you will want to review the study on "joy" as it is expressed by Paul in the Philippian letter in some way. You may want to ask the campers to share insights they have received from the Bible study. The campers may also want to share any creative activity work that they have done during the study. Looking at pictures, letters, prayers, etc. done by the campers will be one of the best ways possible to review learnings and to tie together the entire study.

One way to summarize learnings from the study would be to have campers complete the sentence, "Joy, according to Paul, is. . . ." Or, some campers may like to write a poem using "Joy" as the title.

Close your time together with a prayer. You may voice a prayer using thoughts the campers have expressed in the discussions, or you may use prayers which some of the campers have written during the study.

Part Three
Resources

8
Get-Acquainted Activities

The first few hours in camp are very important. Many of the older elementary children who will be in your group are away from their homes and their families for the first time. Try to do everything possible to make them feel comfortable and welcome at camp. Your activities on the first day will center around getting the campers acquainted with the camp—its facilities and procedures—and with each other and with you.

A tour of the camp is a good way to acquaint the campers with the facilities. As you visit the different parts of camp such as the dining hall and the waterfront area, you can explain the procedures that are in operation in these areas. If the responsible staff persons are on hand in these areas, then they can explain the proper procedures to follow.

After all of your campers have arrived, you will need to have an orientation session. State any special rules of the camp and your expectations of the campers. They appreciate knowing what the rules are and generally want to follow them.

Conversation with campers as they arrive and get settled in their shelters will help you get to know each other. When your small group gets together for the first time, you will need to use a get-acquainted activity or game to help the girls and boys get to know one another. Here are some suggestions.

I'm Going to Camp

One camper or counselor makes the statement, "My name is

_____." *(Fill in the first name.)* "I'm going to camp, and I'm going to take a _____." *(Fill in a noun beginning with the same letter as their first name.)* The second camper says the name of the first person and what that person is taking to camp and then repeats the sentence, "My name is _____. I'm going to camp, and I'm going to take a _____." Keep on until you have gone around the circle. Each person repeats the name of each person who has already spoken and what each is taking to camp. The repetition of names helps campers learn them quickly.

Dyads

Ask each camper to choose a partner and tell that partner three interesting things about himself or herself. After a few moments of conversation, the campers introduce their partners to the group by telling the three interesting facts.

Rhythm

Form a circle with the leader in the center. Clap hands and snap fingers in rhythm: *clap, clap, snap* right, *snap* left. When the rhythm is established, the leader calls his or her own name on the first snap, another player's name on the second snap. The player called must repeat the process, calling a different name. For example, "*clap, clap,* Fred, Sally!" and then "*clap, clap,* Sally, Paul!" A player who breaks the rhythm or fails to call a name becomes the leader. When the leader makes a mistake, he or she drops out of the game.

"About Me" Posters

Give the campers sheets of white tag board or construction paper. Let them show as many things about themselves on the paper as they want to. They can draw pictures or symbols, write words, or use magazine pictures if available. Let all of the campers explain their finished posters to the total group.

Who Are Your Neighbors?

The players sit or stand in a circle. "It," who stands in the middle, will suddenly point to a player and ask, "Who are your neighbors?" The player must answer correctly, giving the names of the players on either side, before "It" can count to ten. A player who misses becomes "It."

9
Campcraft Skills

One feature of your camp program, which will be new and exciting to most of your campers, is the learning and use of camping and outdoor living skills. The discussion that follows will help you see the place of such activities in the overall camp program.

The Small Group Living Area

One of the important elements in your overall camp program will be the development of a small group living area where your group can live, work, study, worship, and play each day. The development of such an area will give your group the opportunity to learn and practice many camping and outdoor living skills. Also it will provide the context for learning about and practicing good principles of ecology and environmental stewardship.

In many camps, small group living areas have already been selected and partially developed, and an area will be assigned to your small group when camp opens. You and your boys and girls will enjoy visiting the site and deciding on ways to improve it and make it more comfortable and attractive. This may involve nothing other than repairing a table and replenishing the woodpile, but it may involve constructing new equipment. Impress upon the group the fact that other campers have worked hard to develop the campsite and have left it in good condition for them. Encourage them to leave the site in even better condition for those who follow.

In other camps, you will need to choose and develop your small group living area. The site should be chosen carefully. It should be accessible to your sleeping shelters, but it should be far enough away from other groups to allow some privacy. There should be sufficient flat ground for the group

to engage in its activities, but the area should be high enough for adequate drainage. There should be trees available to provide shade, but there should be enough open space overhead so that it will be safe to build fires. Firewood should be available if you plan to use it for cooking or for campfires. It is helpful if there is water close by to use for washing hands and dishes, for cooking, and for use in craft projects. (Care should be taken to assure that the water supply is safe to use for drinking and cooking.)

There are virtually unlimited possibilities of ways to develop your small group living area. The sketch of a well-developed living area and the list below will give you and your campers many ideas about how you can develop your own area. For directions on the campcraft skills needed to complete these projects, consult Catherine Hammett's book, *Your Own Book of Campcraft,* or another good campcraft skills book.

Possible projects which will help develop the small group living area include the following: (1) Construct a fire circle. (2) Gather wood and prepare a woodpile. (3) Lash tables and benches. (4) Prepare handwashing facilities. (5) Prepare a shelter if it is needed. (6) Prepare a tool rack to keep tools off the ground and in a safe place.

Remember that camping skills are an important part of a camping program, but they are just one element in the overall program. So you and your campers must be sure that these activities do not monopolize too much of your time. The development of a small group living area is not an end in itself, but is done so that you can have a comfortable and adequate setting for many of your activities.

Remember also that older elementary boys and girls are comparatively inexperienced in camping skills. Do not try to introduce the more difficult and intricate skills before the campers are ready. Help the campers select activities that they can learn easily, and be sure to prepare them for each activity before they begin doing it. Help them limit the number of projects so they can do a good job on those they choose to work on.

Finally, do not feel that you must complete construction of all of your facilities and projects on the first day. Actually it is better if the work is spread out over a number of days. Do first those things that are most essential and then enjoy making other additions throughout the week. Remind the campers that they are not only building for themselves but for those who follow, if the area is to be left for other groups to use.

It may be necessary in a camp with limited land area to restore the small group living area to its natural state at the end of your camp. If so, the development of the site should be limited to only those projects which are absolutely essential for the life and work of your small group.

REJOICING WITH CREATION

10
Outdoor Cooking

Cooking a meal out-of-doors is an excellent group activity, and it is also one that is very enjoyable for older elementary campers. You will want to plan to cook a minimum of one or two meals with your small group.

A successful cookout requires a lot of careful planning and a great deal of time. You will want to keep these things in mind as you plan your cookout:

1. Plan a menu that is balanced but that does not require cooking skills and techniques beyond the level of your campers.

2. Stay within the budget limitations of your camp.

3. Consider the kind of cooking equipment and utensils needed.

4. Consider the type of fire(s) needed and the kind of wood needed. Consult Catherine Hammett's *Your Own Book of Campcraft* for suggestions about the kinds of fires needed for various kinds of cooking.

5. When preparing your food order, be very specific about what it is you want. Do not assume that the persons preparing your order will know what you want.

6. Plan to involve all of the campers in your group in the actual preparation of the meal. You will want to organize them into three groups—fire builders, cooks, cleanup crew. Assign everyone to one of the three groups.

The following types of cooking are most appropriate with older elementary campers and their limited cooking skills:

1. Cooking on a stick
2. One-pot meals such as spaghetti or campfire stew
3. Baking in a dutch oven
4. Cooking in aluminum foil, such as barbecue chicken or vegetables.

Limit the number of items on your menu which must actually be cooked. You will need to determine how many fires you will need by the number of dishes to be cooked at a given meal.

Some sample recipes are given below. These are all appropriate with older elementary campers. Add other recipes of your own to the list.

Campfire Stew *(serves 12)*

>   3 lbs. of hamburger steak
>   2 large onions, peeled and diced
>   1 tbsp. fat
>   3 (10 oz.) cans concentrated vegetable soup
>   salt and pepper

Make little balls of hamburger, adding seasoning. Fry with onions in a frying pan or in the bottom of a kettle until onion is light brown and balls are well-browned all over. Pour off excess fat. Add vegetable soup and enough water or soup stock to prevent sticking. Cover and stir occasionally. Cook slowly until meat balls are cooked through. Serve hot.

Come Again Spaghetti *(serves 10-12)*

>   3 lbs. hamburger
>   ¼ lb. bacon
>   4 no. 2 cans spaghetti in tomato sauce
>   2 onions
>   salt and pepper
>   ¼ lb. American cheese

Fry bacon until crisp and put in kettle. Fry the onions in bacon grease until golden brown. Add to the kettle. Brown hamburger and put in kettle along with the spaghetti, salt, and pepper. Simmer fifteen minutes. If too thick, add water. Cut the cheese into small cubes and stir in until cheese is soft. Remove from fire and serve immediately.

Barbequed Chicken *(serves 12)*

    4-5 onions sliced thin
    1 tsp. dry mustard *or* 3 tsp. prepared mustard
    ¼ cup brown sugar
    salt and pepper
    ¼ cup vinegar
    ¾ cup catsup
    1 cup water (use more if needed to cover chicken)
    2 tbsp. Worcestershire sauce
    2 chickens, cut up, or 12 leg-thighs

Place all ingredients in a Dutch oven with chicken and bring to a boil. Continue to cook over low fire until chicken is tender. Brown on grill over coals if desired.

Ground Meat with Vegetables *(serves 12)*

    2½ lbs. ground steak or hamburger
    sliced onions, potatoes, carrots (approximately 12 each)
    butter
    salt and pepper

Arrange slices of potato, onion, and carrot on a large square of aluminum foil. Place a pattie of ground meat on the top. Cover with more vegetables. Salt and pepper to taste. Dot with butter. Wrap securely in foil and cook over hot coals. Turn frequently to prevent burning.

Vegetable Salad

    1 large head lettuce, washed
    2 tomatoes, cubed
    celery and cucumbers as desired

Tear lettuce into small pieces and combine with tomatoes, celery, and cucumbers. Add three-fourths cup French or Italian dressing.

Waldorf Salad *(serves 12)*

    2 cups diced celery
    2 cups diced apples
    ½ cup pecans
    ¾ cup mayonnaise

Combine all of the ingredients and serve on a lettuce leaf.

Carrot and Raisin Salad *(serves 12)*

    8 large carrots
    1 cup seedless raisins
    1 cup coarsely chopped pecans or peanuts (optional)
    1 tsp. salt
    mayonnaise or dressing (as below)

Scrape the carrots well and place them on ice for an hour. Then grate them coarsely into a bowl. Add the other ingredients and toss with mayonnaise or sour cream dressing.

Sour Cream Dressing

    1 tbsp. grated lemon peel
    2 tbsp. lemon juice
    1 cup sour cream

Mix together ingredients and serve over salad.

Mock Angel Cake *(serves 12)*

    1 loaf of bread, unsliced or thick-sliced (day-old bread is best)
    1 cup sweetened condensed milk
    1 box shredded coconut

Trim crust off the bread. Cut into cubes one and one-half to two inches square. Place bread on a sharpened stick and dip quickly into the condensed milk and cover with coconut. Toast over coals.

Banana Boats

    1 banana for each person
    1 bag of miniature marshmallows
    1/3 plain Hershey bar for each person or ½ lb. sweet chocolate bits for 12

With a sharp knife carefully lay back a lengthwise section of banana peeling. Do not cut it off. Remove a lengthwise wedge of banana. Insert small chocolate pieces and marshmallows. Cover with the peeling and use a toothpick to secure. Place on a low rack over coals and cook until the banana peeling turns brown. Delicious, but rich! Banana boats cook in about 15 minutes.

Applesauce and Gingerbread *(serves 12)*

    6 cups applesauce
    1 box gingerbread mix

    Heat the applesauce in a Dutch oven. Mix the gingerbread batter, following the directions on the box. When the sauce is hot, pour the batter on top, taking care not to disturb the applesauce. Cover tightly with a lid. If the lid does not fit tightly, place foil on top and then replace the lid. Simmer on hot coals for 30 minutes. Since gingerbread is to steam, avoid the temptation to take a look until the 30 minutes are up.

Some-Mores *(serves 12)*

    24 graham crackers
    12 marshmallows
    24 pieces milk chocolate candy

    Place two pieces of milk chocolate on a graham cracker. Toast a marshmallow; place it on top of the chocolate. Cover with a second cracker.

11
Explorations and Discoveries

It is possible for campers to spend a week or more at camp and never get in touch with the beauty and wonder of God's world. As a counselor, you need to plan for some experiences that will help your campers begin to appreciate the world about them.

Above all, you should exhibit an attitude that encourages campers to really enjoy the world. Encourage the members of your group to take the time to soak in the sunshine or see the stars or hear the birds or feel the rain. Encourage them to take the time to explore and discover. The world is worth the time we give to really enjoy it!

The activities described below are just a few of the many activities that can help you get your campers in touch with the world. Use this list to stimulate your own thinking.

Study a Stump

Select a tree that has fallen or has been cut and study the stump. See if the campers are able to answer such questions as: (1) What kind of tree was this? (2) How old do you think the tree was when it fell or was cut? (3) If the tree was cut, what tool was used to cut it? (4) Why was the tree cut? (5) In what direction did the tree fall? (Look for some clues—splinters left on the stump, chips of wood or sawdust around the tree.)

Choosing a Favorite Tree

Early in your camp session, suggest that each person select a tree to enjoy and to study. After the campers have had two or three days to look at their tree and have had an opportunity to learn as much as they can about it, ask them to either write a brief description of the tree or tell the group about the tree. This could include where the tree is, what it looks like, the kind of tree it is, the color and texture of the bark, its nuts and fruits (if any), etc. Each camper may choose to draw pictures of the tree, to make up a riddle about the tree, to make a spatter print of the leaves, or to show appreciation for this "favorite" tree in some way.

Getting to Know a Tree (an Acclimatization exercise)

Put blindfolds on your campers to heighten their other senses. After a short spin to erase the sense of direction, guide each camper to a tree. Ask the camper to explore that tree. Hug it. Rub his or her cheek against it. Listen to it—try to hear the life inside it, the sap running, the life breathing within. Explore its "skin" with tongue, fingers, nose, skin. Check out its base—where it grows. Is anything living on it? After the campers get to know their trees, lead them away again. Then, take the blindfolds off, return to the general area. and let the campers try to find their same trees again. They probably will. Very soon each camper will be heard to exclaim, "This is mine!"

Star Viewing

Let the campers stay up a little later one night to view the stars. Lie down in an open field and look up. See the stars as a canopy. Then, focus on one individual star for a time. Finally, look for patterns in the stars. Having a guide to the stars available will allow you to locate some of the major constellations.

Symphony (an Acclimatization exercise)

Have your campers lie down like the spokes of a wheel with their feet in the center. Ask them to close their eyes and just listen for a couple of minutes to the various sounds. Try not to identify the sounds, but just let them flow into your mind and blend together, like all the different instruments in a symphony. Instead of naming the sounds, describe them with letters. (For example, "wind" becomes "whhirrrrr.....") Let the sounds move you and maybe even seemingly lift you up to float quietly for a few moments. Do this for a couple of minutes. Then concentrate on the sounds drifting in and fading out—the crescendos and the decrescendos of a symphony orchestra.

Seton Watching (an Acclimatization exercise)

Station each camper in your group in one spot where he or she can sit comfortably for a few moments. Ask the camper to sit perfectly still for about twenty minutes. Tell them to listen and look. In that amount of time, the world will go back to the natural state it was in before being invaded by campers. Ask the campers to share what they saw and heard and felt.

Rain Gauge

A rain gauge is a way of measuring the amount of water that falls during a rain. A simple gauge can be made from a straight-sided, flat-bottomed jar such as a mayonnaise jar. Put it in a level, open place as soon as the rain starts. Measure the inches and fractions of inches of water in the bottom of the jar. Mark on the outside of the jar with a marking pencil or a piece of soap exactly the level of the water. Be as accurate as possible. Empty the jar. Measure the distance from the bottom of the jar to the mark by placing a ruler on the inside of the jar. For your weather record, write down the date and the exact amount of rain.

12
Nature Crafts

Creating something of one's own is an exciting experience for an older elementary camper. The craft program in camp provides campers with the opportunity to do just that.

The crafts suggested here are crafts that utilize primarily materials found in nature. Such crafts allow this phase of the camp program to be co-ordinated with other parts of the program. A hike or ramble through the woods becomes an opportunity to gather materials that will be used later in the campers' creations. Looking around for materials makes the campers more aware of the world around them and the God who created this world.

The actual process of working on the crafts will generally be a small group activity. The activity can be a time of real fellowship as the campers share ideas and materials and lend a hand to their fellow campers.

Spatter Prints of Leaves

Using pins, fasten a leaf to a sheet of paper. Dip a brush in berry juice or paint. Shake off the excess. Take a piece of screen wire and hold it two inches or more above the paper. Rub the brush over the screen wire to make small spatters. Move the screen wire around so that a small spatter of paint is over all the area to be covered. You can use either white paint on dark paper or colored paint on white paper.

Blueprints of Leaves

Place a leaf on a piece of blueprint paper, holding it with a pane of glass. Expose the leaf and paper to the sun until the paper turns light. Develop the blueprint in a pan containing two cups of water and one-half cup of peroxide. Wash the blueprint in clear water and hang it up to dry. Flowers and grasses can also be blueprinted. Attractive prints can be made by arranging flowers and grasses creatively.

Leaf Rubbings

Place a piece of smooth paper over a leaf with the veined side up. Rub a crayon over the paper gently but firmly, making all of your strokes in one direction. The print of the leaf should show up clearly on the paper. This is an excellent way to decorate notepaper or stationery.

Ink Prints

Place a leaf, vein side down, on a stamp pad. Cover the leaf with a sheet of newspaper and press down with your fingers to make sure the leaf makes contact with the stamp pad. Raise the newspaper. Remove the leaf and place it, vein side down, on a piece of white paper. Cover the leaf with a clean piece of newspaper and press gently but firmly with your hand. Lift both paper and leaf, and a dainty print of the leaf is left on the paper. These prints can be used to decorate notepaper or stationery.

Nature Mobiles

Gather small pine cones, acorns, stones, bark, shells, seedpods, etc. and suspend them from a small tree branch with binder twine, string, or thin wire. Be sure to balance the weight so that the tree branch will hang in a horizontal position. The completed mobile can then be hung in the small group living area or inside a building.

Nature Collages

Make a design by attaching all kinds of barks, crushed leaves, stones, shells, vines, dried flowers, etc. to a piece of board or to a piece of cardboard covered with burlap. The completed collage should be sprayed with clear shellac or plastic.

Rock Sculpture

Interesting pieces of sculpture can be made by gluing small stones together into the shapes of animals and other creatures. Rocks may be chipped into pieces or used whole. Use a glue that dries clear.

Clay Modeling

If there is native clay on your campsite, gather some in a bucket or can and cover it with a wet cloth to keep it in a pliable condition. The clay can be formed into all kinds of interesting shapes. Allow the clay figures to dry slowly in a shady place to prevent cracking.

Charcoal Sketching

Save pieces of charcoal from the campfire. Hard woods make the best pieces of charcoal. Sharpen the charcoal with a piece of sandstone and use it to sketch on a piece of paper or on a flat stone.

A Terrarium

Small plants, mosses, and barks or rocks with lichen can be arranged in a glass gallon jar. Turn the jar on its side. Place an inch layer of charcoal in the bottom and then add an inch layer of topsoil. Arrange the plants and barks or rocks. Water carefully and screw on the lid.

Decorated Matchboxes

Cut pieces of felt or burlap to fit the top and bottom of a matchbox. Leave the striking surface uncovered. After the material is glued on the box, arrange small cones, pods, nuts, seashells, or other natural materials on the top of the box.

Paint with Flowers and Grasses

If flowers are abundant in your camp, you may be able to pick some without harm to the world around you. Rub the crushed petals over paper to paint a picture. Grasses and leaves will yield many different shades of greens and browns. Limit the size of the pictures to dimensions of six to eight inches.

13
Games

There are many times during camp when games are appropriate—in the small group living area, on the trail as you hike, in the shelter as you rest after lunch. Play games with a purpose, however. Don't just use them to fill time. Games should be a natural part of your group life.

Choose carefully the games that you play. Use sparingly games which are highly competitive. Remember, you are trying to develop a group, not tear it down. Choose games that challenge each individual to do his or her best. Use variety in your games. Always stop a game while everyone is still enjoying it.

The following games are samples of the many different kinds of games that can be played in the camp setting. You will probably know others to add to this list.

Camp Horseshoes

Cut four "horseshoes" from forked branches from one to one and one-half inches thick. These and a couple of stakes are all that are needed for a game of camp horseshoes.

Ring-on-a-String

Make a ring four or five inches in diameter from a small green branch that is pliable. Tie it with twine. Tie twine to a pointed stick and to the ring.

Swing the ring back and forth and try to catch the ring on the end of the stick.

Hoop Statue

Make a hoop about a foot in diameter from vines. Form a circle with hands joined. "It" stands in the center of the circle. All players take ten steps back from the circle and stand still. They cannot move, but may bend their bodies to get out of the way of the hoop. Whoever "It" hits when he or she throws the hoop becomes the new "It." If "It" does not succeed in hitting anyone, all of the players may run around, dodging "It" until he or she does hit someone with the hoop.

Categories

Give each person a piece of paper and a pencil. Have them write down these categories and letters (or use the name of your camp):

	Animals	Trees	Birds	Flowers
C				
A				
M				
P				

Give the group five minutes to fill in as many blocks as possible—one point for each block correctly filled in. Vary the game by using new letters and categories.

Nature Alphabet

Divide your group in half and choose a leader for each group. Each leader is given paper and pencil. He or she lists the letters of the alphabet down the left side of the page. At the given signal both groups hunt for nature objects in the surrounding area that begin with the various letters. Only one object is named for each letter. General classification names cannot be used. For instance, pine may be used for "P" but not tree for "T."

When ten minutes have elapsed, call the two groups back to see which one has the most items named.

Find the Leader

The group forms a circle. One person leaves the circle, and a person is chosen to be the leader. As "It" returns to the group, the leader and group begin clapping hands. The leader changes motions as often and as unobtrusively as possible. When "It" discovers the person responsible for making the different motions, someone else is chosen to be "It."

Squirrel in the Tree

This game is played with groups of four. Three players join hands and form a small circle. This is the tree. The fourth player stands in the center, as the squirrel. Two extra players are a squirrel and a hound. The hound chases the squirrel, who darts into a tree for safety. The squirrel already in the tree must get out and dart into another tree. If the hound catches a squirrel outside a tree, that squirrel becomes the hound, and the hound becomes a squirrel.

Nature Sounds

The group halts and keeps perfectly quiet for five mintues. Each person then lists all the sounds heard during the silence. The longest list wins. The list will vary considerably, and the group will enjoy seeing how many sounds they hear.

14
Campfires

Camp and campfires are almost synonymous, for camp would not be camp without a campfire and the fun and fellowship that accompany the campfire program. Some of the most memorable experiences of camp are those which take place around the campfire.

You will certainly want to plan for several campfires with your older elementary campers. Generally, the campfire will be an experience of your small group, although at times your group may want to invite another group to join you for a campfire and refreshments, or there may be a large campfire for the entire camp.

The campfire setting is a good one for getting acquainted on the first evening and for drawing your camp experience to a close. And campfires are good fun on any nights between the first and the last.

What do you do around the campfire? The possibilities are varied. Singing is always popular—fun songs, motion songs, folk songs, spirituals, and hymns all have their place in the campfire program. Stunts and skits are fun to use, particularly group stunts and participation stunts that involve the entire group. Storytelling and campfires go hand in hand. Refreshments seem to taste better around the campfire, particularly if you take advantage of the fire to roast marshmallows or pop popcorn.

There is no better setting than around a campfire for making plans for the next day or for talking about problems and situations that have arisen during the day. Worship is always a fitting climax to the campfire program.

Plan carefully for your campfire programs. They just may be the high points of the camp session for you and your campers.

15
Songs and Music

Singing is an important and happy part of a camp experience. Singing can be enjoyed any time and any place—along a trail, at the small group living area, around the campfire, as the grace before a meal, or during a time of worship. Every counselor needs to be prepared to lead the small group in singing and in other types of musical expression. Don't deny your campers the joy of singing just because you don't feel you sing well enough to lead others. You don't have to know how to sing well in order to help other people enjoy singing.

Much of the singing that your small group will do will start spontaneously as you and your campers sit around a campfire, rest on a hike, or work on a project. As a counselor, you must be prepared to assist your group in choosing songs that are wholesome and that express the right attitudes about people.

It is not necessary to have songbooks in order to sing. If you plan to introduce a large number of new songs, you may want to duplicate the words or write them on a large poster board. Children learn quickly through repetition, however, so printing the words is not necessary if you will sing the songs several times during the camp session.

The following steps may be helpful when you are teaching a song to your group:

1. Sing the song through by yourself or with those in the group who know it.

2. Next, teach the song to the group by rote—one line at a time. You sing a line, and then they sing it.
3. Then, put the song together. Sing it through several times so that the group can become more and more familiar with the song and can begin to enjoy it.
4. Use the song again and again during the camp session.

There are a number of small, pocket-size songbooks available which contain good songs for use in camp. You may want to bring one or two along with you. And you will certainly want to make lists of appropriate songs to sing during camp. List them in categories such as fun songs, rounds, motion songs, campfire songs, hiking songs, folk songs, spirituals, and hymns.

Every small group should also have available a copy of your denomination's hymnal to use in worship. Words of hymns may be read as calls to worship, as prayers, or as responses, in addition to being sung. As your campers plan for worship experiences, you will want to help them select hymns that support the theme of the service.

You may want to help your group create a new stanza to an existing hymn. Or, you can create an entirely new hymn which can be sung to a familiar tune or to a new tune which the group can compose.

BIBLIOGRAPHY

Some of the resources listed are out of print but may be available in your local, camp, or church library.

CAMP ADMINISTRATION AND PHILOSOPHY

Davis, Robert P. *Church Camping.* Richmond, Virginia: John Knox Press, 1969.

Creative Church Camping. Philadelphia: Lutheran Church Press, 1971.

Johnson, Ronald K. *Planning Outdoor Christian Education.* Philadelphia: United Church Press, 1972.

Purchase, Richard and Betty. *Let's Go Outdoors with Children.* Philadelphia: Westminster Press, 1972.

Witt, Ted R. *Toward Excellence in Church Camping.* Nashville: Discipleship Resources, 1974.

WORSHIP RESOURCES

Brandt, Leslie F. *Psalms/Now.* St. Louis: Concordia Publishing House, 1973.

Bowman, Clarice M. *Worship Ways for Camp.* New York: Association Press, 1955.

MacInnes, Gordon A. *A Guide To Worship in Camp and Conference.* Philadelphia: Westminster Press, 1962.

ARTS AND CRAFTS

Hammett, Catherine T., and Harrocks, Carol M. *Creative Crafts for Campers.* New York: Association Press, 1957.

Musselman, Virginia. *Learning About Nature Through Crafts.* Harrisburg, Pennsylvania: Stackpole Company, 1969.

Stinson, Thelma. *Native 'N' Creative.* Nashville: Methodist Board of Education, 1957.

RECREATION

Bannerman, Glenn, and Fakkema, Robert. *Guide for Recreation Leaders.* Atlanta: John Knox Press, 1975.

Fluegelman, Andrew, ed. *The New Games Book.* New York: Doubleday, 1976.

Musselman, Virginia. *Learning About Nature Through Games.* Harrisburg, Pennsylvania: Stackpole Company, 1967.

CAMPCRAFT

Hammett, Catherine. *Your Own Book of Campcraft.* New York: Pocket Books, 1950.

NATURE AND ECOLOGY

Golden Nature Guide Series. New York: Golden Press.
Titles available include:

Birds	Spiders and Their Kin
Fishes	Trees
Fossils	Weeds
Geology	Butterflies and Moths
Insects	Flowers
Nonflowering Plants	Game Birds
Reptiles and Amphibians	Insect Pests
Mammals	Pond Life
Rocks and Minerals	Stars
Weather	Zoology

Storer, John H. *The Web of Life.* New York: New American Library, 1972.

Van Matre, Steve. *Acclimatization.* Martinsville, Indiana: American Camping Association, 1972.

Van Matre, Steve. *Acclimatizing.* American Camping Association, 1974.

STORIES

Chase, Richard. *American Folk Tales and Songs.* New York: Dover Pubns., 1971.

Chase, Richard. *Grandfather Tales.* Boston: Houghton Mifflin Co., 1948.

Chase, Richard. *Jack Tales.* Boston: Houghton Mifflin Co., 1943.

Kuntz, Bob. *Stories You Can Tell.* Nashville: Discipleship Resources, 1977.

Bell, Martin. *The Way of the Wolf.* New York: Seabury Press, 1970.

Bell, Martin. *Nenshu and the Tiger.* New York: Seabury Press, 1975.

Notes

1. Robert Davis, *Church Camping* (Richmond, Virginia: John Knox Press, 1969), p. 12.
2. Howard E. Walker, *Teaching Yourself to Teach* Kit (Nashville: Abingdon Press, 1974).
3. From *Handle with Care* Resource Packet, Grades 5-6 (Vacation Ventures Series, Cooperative Publication Association, © 1974).